HEMINGWAY

A LIFE IN PICTURES

BORIS VEJDOVSKY WITH
MARIEL HEMINGWAY

FIREFLY BOOKS

HE
MING-
WAY

A gentleman, a hunter, a deep-sea fisherman, a lover of food and fine wine, a man of precise words and my grandfather. "Papa" died before I was born, three months to be exact, yet my whole life has been a reflection of how creative and powerful my grandfather's legacy is to my life and to the lives of those around me. There is not a day that passes where I am not reminded of his talents, his strength and his ability to touch the lives of millions around the world. He changed the way American writers write and is still important to lovers of literature everywhere. There is a fascination with the purity of his storytelling and a longing by many artists to live an extraordinary life, whether in France, Cuba, Spain, Italy, Florida or Idaho. He was an adventurer who still inspires us today.

My father, Jack, Ernest's first son, took me to Paris when I was 10 years old, and we read *A Moveable Feast* together while my father walked me around this magical city and showed me where he had been brought up. We rode bikes and traveled around like my dad had done with his father — we biked through the Tuileries, past Papa's first apartment and where Papa looked at Cézanne's pears for the first time. We bought a book from the Sylvia Beach bookstore and looked at Ernest's titles alongside his mentors James Joyce, F. Scott Fitzgerald and Balzac, among others. Paris was where Ernest became a writer. He left the States to challenge himself to be better, bigger and to live more fully. In Paris, he was hungry, passionate and driven to become exceptional. When you go there and visit his haunts or simply walk the streets, you can feel his energy in the breath of the city. You can feel why he loved to write with the scent of wet cobblestones, fresh croissants and café crèmes in the hands of stunning women at a sidewalk café. He loved the richness of life.

I understand his appreciation for the best of the best. Whether it was the best fly-fishing stream, the best Bordeaux or the most beautiful woman in the room, my grandfather knew what was great. He wanted to experience it, taste it, feel it and stand in the face of anything that stretched him beyond the limits of his own comfort. He felt that facing talent, power and danger is what brought out the excellence in a man. He knew that a person becomes more by experiencing something extraordinary.

I love being Ernest Hemingway's granddaughter because I feel that I have been given a gift of seeing the remarkable things that life has to offer. Papa loved nature, simplicity, food and people. He gleaned the exceptional from them. I have taken that into my heart and thank him daily for making me able to see how incredibly intricate the simplest of things can be. Whether it is the tea I drink in the morning or the breeze that comes when there is a hint of autumn in the air in the mountains of Idaho, I see things differently because of where I come from and the blood that comes from my grandfather. He is in my blood, he is my legacy and I am honored to be a part of him.

Mariel Hemingway

White beard, an insolent stare masking a gentleness behind the eyes, a craggy bear's face: the ultimate cliché of a writer-adventurer. Worse, a sepia photo stuck in the album of a scout dreaming of pretend glories! And his life ... a good boys' adventure novel that has it all: a naturally courageous ambulance driver wounded on the Italian front of the First World War; a disillusioned journalist in Paris, with Fitzgerald and others, between two worldwide conflicts; hunter of wild animals at the foot of Kilimanjaro; frequenter of bars in Cuba; ringside bullfighter in Spain; keeper of six-toed cats in Key West; tracker of trout in the cool, shaded rivers of Michigan; and part-time American spy, scouring the warm waters of the Gulf Stream in his fishing boat for German submarines — an old man on the sea.

Loving Hemingway? Paying him homage 50 years after his death? What is the point? Such creatures do not exist any more. He is a specimen stored away in some forgotten gallery of the Museum of Mankind. A Yankee mummy frozen in another age, when the land was still untainted. Wild territories explored on foot, horseback or canoe in the footsteps of a doctor father who treated trappers and Indian tribes as he wandered through the untouched forests of North America. This was a boy who had no time for the invading polluters: vandals who, he believed, betrayed the land that had given birth to them. A land that he no longer recognized. Only Idaho, in the northwest of the United States, where he put two rifle bullets in his head one quiet July morning in 1961, allowed him to relive the distant memories of his Illinois boyhood. Love old Ernest? What madness!

Strange, then, that such a man should still have such an impact today. Does our fractured humanity need strong paternal figures to emerge from its apathy? On Sunday mornings we can fantasize that we are free and spirited adventurers, but at the first light of dawn on Monday, we are back to our dull lives. Do we need to hear the cruel judgment on our lives given in the form of an homage paid by an admirer named Marlene Dietrich, "The most remarkable thing about Ernest is that he has found time to do the things most men only dream about"? For whom does the bell toll? For all of us, struggling against time.

Through his zest and daring, Hemingway makes us regret all the more our abandoned ambitions, our forgotten promises — above all, the ones that transcend our limits — our easy renunciations, our betrayed passions, our vivid fears — living, loving, dying. Will we ever be Robert Jordan, putting our ideals above everything else? Will we leave the warm comfort of our easy lives to fight for our convictions far from home? Plunged in the pages of his novels, we feel ourselves capable of it. But once the book is closed, where will we get our inspiration from? To live like the wild beasts of the savannah, bulls of the arena or men on the battlefield? The same struggle, the eternal confrontation between life and death. Story after story, we tap into this wild intensity, these passions given free expression, all that could give meaning to our lives. No longer just dreaming about them but simply living them! And so old Ernest is more relevant than ever in our dulled society, fed by turgid debate, in which restraint takes priority over action. These lost heroes give us renewed hope and courage.

Pierre Fery-Zendel

To the insolent muses
"Life is the reflection of literature."
Wallace Stevens

More than any other 20th century author, Ernest Hemingway transformed the world he lived in and the landscape of Anglo-American and world literature. His characters, who reflected and transcended the man and the public character he constructed, gave him an aura that very few of his contemporaries would attain. Writing would transform the landscapes of the life and fiction of Ernest Hemingway into lands both strange and familiar.

This book commemorates the 50th anniversary of the death of a figure known even by those who have never read him. Even though it is sometimes difficult to distinguish Ernest's characters from the man himself, one should not avoid taking a detour into his fiction when attempting to reconstruct his life. Nick Adams, the hero of numerous stories, Frederick Henry of *A Farewell to Arms*, Robert Jordan of *For Whom the Bell Tolls*, Jake Barnes of *The Sun Also Rises*, right up to Santiago in *The Old Man and the Sea* — they all contain something of Ernest. However, the question is not so much that of knowing to what extent these characters resemble him as of understanding to what extent he resembles them. This is not simply some anachronistic paradox: we cannot cling to the common-sense notion that Hemingway the author necessarily preceded his creations. We gain access to Ernest Hemingway only through his fiction.

If we think that Ernest's writing is a simple transformation of his life story, we are mistaken. And so, his professed aversion to his mother might be nothing more than a trivial adolescent reaction if it were not inscribed into our reading of stories such as "The Doctor and the Doctor's Wife" or "Fathers and Sons." In the same way, Grace's admittedly rather unusual style of child rearing — which made her treat Ernest and his older sister as "twins" — would be nothing more than a passing oddity if Hemingway's fiction did not explore, in repeated and almost obsessive fashion, the themes of the female reflected in the masculine, twinship, transvestism and confusion of gender. When Kenneth Lynn, one of Ernest's biographers, assures us that his mother "cherished the hope that Ernest's hair would remain blond," was he reading history or fiction? The reader would rediscover these themes, including that of blondness shared by a man and a woman, from *The Sun Also Rises* to the posthumous *The Garden of Eden*, a novel in which these questions explode with a complexity that carries the life and the work away in one and the same whirlwind. How, therefore, not to read Ernest as the descendant of David Bourne in *The Garden of Eden*, how not to see the paradise lost of the latter as the retrospective announcement of the loss of innocence of the former? How not to read what Kenneth Lynn calls Ernest's "Edenic infancy" as the reflection of his prose in *The Garden of Eden*?

We are all Hemingway's readers, and the only access we have to him is through writing, his writing.

INDIAN CAMP

An American Childhood

The family home, situated at 439 North Oak Park Avenue in Oak Park, Illinois, looks like any other middle-class American house. However, the birth there on July 21, 1899, of Ernest, the second child of Dr. Clarence Hemingway and his wife, Grace, would give the residence a reputation and aura that would distinguish it from all the others in the neighborhood, and even the country. In his 62 years of existence, Ernest Hemingway would transform the places of his life into unique landscapes, mythical realms in which fiction and lived experience combined, sometimes indistinguishably.

Opposite page: The house where Ernest was born, 439 North Oak Park Avenue, now a museum.

1. Ernest and his sisters in 1906. From left to right: Marcelline, Madelaine (known as "Sunny") on her father's knee, Ursula with her mother, and Ernest.

2. December 1899. Ernest at six months.

3. January 1901. Eighteen months old: Ernest dressed as a little girl by his mother.

4. One of the first photos in which he poses as a "real" boy. He is five years and three months old.

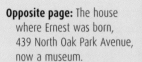

Ernest Miller Hemingway was born and grew up some 12 miles (20 km) from Chicago, the Windy City. With its religious and cultural conservatism, however, Oak Park was very far removed from its cosmopolitan, worldly and turbulent neighbor. Ernest was brought up with deep values, similar to those in the famous childhood of Henry Adams, loyalty to which, it was drummed into him, would bring him success in any domain. Oak Park was a place of abstinence; there was no alcohol there. There was also no racial or religious mixing, with no blacks and few Jews. The town, nicknamed "Saint's Rest," certainly numbered many churches but only one was Catholic.

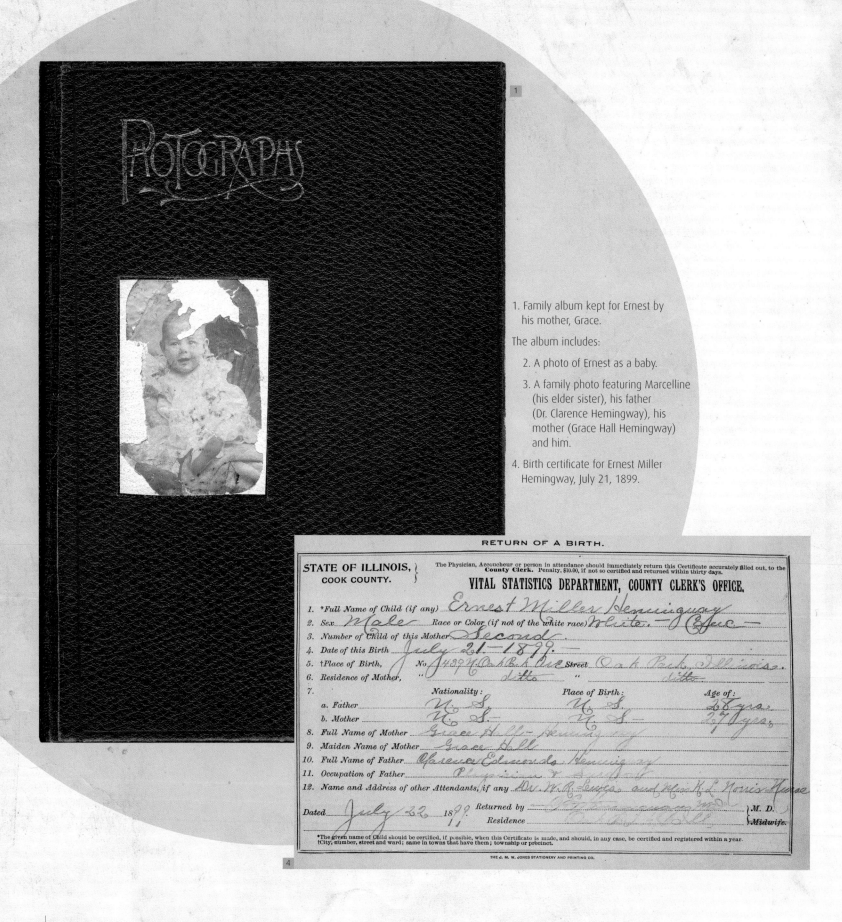

1. Family album kept for Ernest by his mother, Grace.

The album includes:

2. A photo of Ernest as a baby.

3. A family photo featuring Marcelline (his elder sister), his father (Dr. Clarence Hemingway), his mother (Grace Hall Hemingway) and him.

4. Birth certificate for Ernest Miller Hemingway, July 21, 1899.

RETURN OF A BIRTH.

STATE OF ILLINOIS,
COOK COUNTY.

The Physician, Accoucheur or person in attendance should immediately return this Certificate accurately filled out, to the County Clerk. Penalty, $10.00, if not so certified and returned within thirty days.

VITAL STATISTICS DEPARTMENT, COUNTY CLERK'S OFFICE.

1. *Full Name of Child (if any) *Ernest Miller Hemingway*
2. Sex *Male* Race or Color (if not of the white race) *White. — Office —*
3. Number of Child of this Mother *Second*
4. Date of this Birth *July 21 - 1899*
5. †Place of Birth, No *439 N Oak Park Ave* Street *Oak Park Illinois*
6. Residence of Mother, " *ditto* " *ditto*
7. Nationality: Place of Birth: Age of:
   a. Father *U.S.* *U.S.* *38 yrs*
   b. Mother *U.S.* *U.S.* *27 yrs*
8. Full Name of Mother *Grace Hall Hemingway*
9. Maiden Name of Mother *Grace Hall*
10. Full Name of Father *Clarence Edwards Hemingway*
11. Occupation of Father *Physician & Author*
12. Name and Address of other Attendants, if any *Dr. W. R. Lewis and Miss K. L. Morris Nurse*

Dated *July 22* 18*99* Returned by _____ M. D.
Residence _____ Midwife.

*The given name of Child should be certified, if possible, when this Certificate is made, and should, in any case, be certified and registered within a year.
†City, number, street and ward; same in towns that have them; township or precinct.

THE J. M. W. JONES STATIONERY AND PRINTING CO.

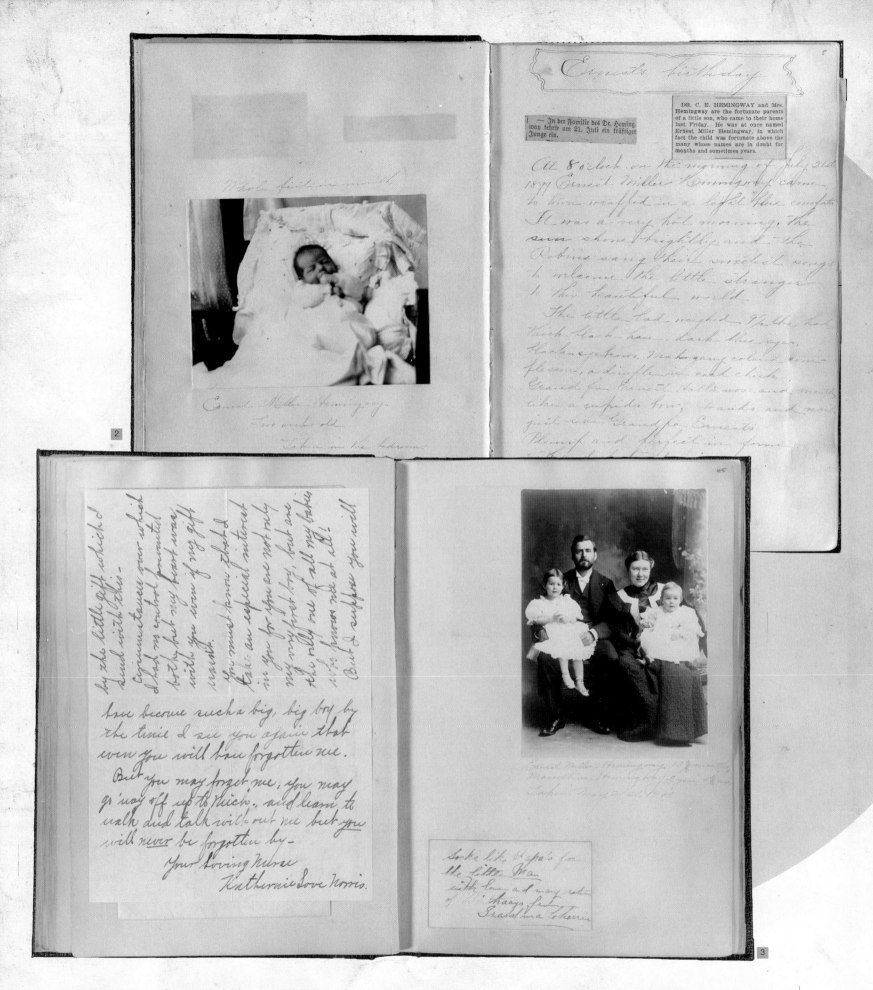

An American Childhood

The cultural and architectural landscape of Ernest's immediate surroundings contained nothing out of the ordinary. However, the Hemingways lived a few blocks from the famous architect Frank Lloyd Wright, figurehead of the so-called Prairie School, a forerunner of Bauhaus. Adherents of the Prairie style produced organic buildings with low horizontal lines and basic geometrical shapes. Ernest often visited one of these houses, belonging to his uncle George, a character who would later appear in the story "Indian Camp." The Hemingways' house exemplified the European taste adopted by inhabitants on the outskirts of Chicago; after the great Chicago fire of 1871, this trend was favored over the more typically American-style wooden houses.

1. Natural landscape of Ernest's childhood in Oak Park.

2, 3. Ernest was born at the convergence of two worlds: the rural American world (left, a building being constructed by a traditional method) and the modernism of the 20th century (right, the house of architect Frank Lloyd Wright).

Right page: Ernest fishing in Horton Creek; he is five years old. This photo, taken by his father, was long kept within the family.

On the death of Hemingway's maternal grandfather in 1905, and with a growing family (Marcelline, 1898; Ernest, 1899; Ursula, 1902; Madelaine, 1904) to accommodate, Grace Hemingway decided to use her inheritance, sell the house and build a bigger home a short distance away. This would also allow Clarence to establish a medical practice on the premises and Grace to flatter her artist's ego, as testified by the magnificent music room that she later added. Although it would be far fetched to claim that the architecture of the period had a lasting influence on Ernest, it can be said that Hemingway's plain, almost geometrically sparse style has something in common with the purified architecture characteristic of the Prairie School. As Ernest wrote in *Death in the Afternoon:* "Prose is architecture, not interior decoration, and the Baroque is over."

Opposite page: Ernest, hunter in the grass, 1906.

1. Anson Hemingway, Ernest's paternal grandfather, mentioned in *For Whom the Bell Tolls.*

2. Music room added by Grace to the Hemingways' new home, at 600 North Kenilworth Avenue.

Below: Ernest, February 1916.

It is not entirely certain whether Ernest did indeed say that Oak Park was composed of "wide lawns and narrow minds," but this remark, however apocryphal, is an apt description of the town and its influence on him. It is also a reflection of the personality that Ernest would construct for himself and that would be constructed for him. Although some of his biographers — and Ernest himself — would try to portray him as a rebel, contemporary testimonies point to a Hemingway who was more Benjamin Franklin than Tom Sawyer: he was a good pupil and regularly attended church, where he sang — albeit without much enthusiasm — in the choir. Writing would certainly take Ernest from the strict Protestantism of his childhood, but there is nothing to suggest that his piety was lacking at that time. His school career was similarly well disciplined and assiduous. A voracious reader (just like his sister Marcelline), he adopted Oak Park's Anglophilia in books ranging from Shakespeare to Dickens. He read little American literature, although it is no surprise to find *The Adventures of Huckleberry Finn* and the president-hunter Theodore Roosevelt's *African Game Trails* among his favorite books. Ernest's exemplary record culminated in his being chosen by his teachers to give his graduation day commencement speech on June 13, 1917. He refused, however, to go on to university, choosing instead to orient himself toward writing, at first through journalism.

The two opposing forces in young Ernest's life, embodied by his mother, Grace, and his father, Clarence, represented sensibilities that would never leave him and that would continually throw off the compass of his writing life. His mother had inclinations toward art and music. A singer, she had had her heart set on the stage before marrying Clarence, and she inculcated her children with a taste for fine arts and music. Ernest's sisters were particular victims of Grace's frustration, Marcelline and Ernest even being taken out of school for a year to devote themselves to singing and the cello. Ernest, for many years the Hemingways' sole male child, did not escape the influence of a mother who was both progressive and dominating. He was taken on annual pilgrimages to the Art Institute of Chicago, where he discovered several famous paintings by artists whose works he would later go to see, like old friends, in museums all over the world, in particular the Prado in Madrid and the Louvre in Paris. He was especially enamored of the stuffed African animals in the Museum of Natural History, linking them to essays and newspaper articles recounting the 1909 safari of Theodore "Teddy" Roosevelt, whom he much admired. Grace also took her children to Nantucket, on the Atlantic coast. In 1910 it was Ernest's turn, and this journey would be the inspiration for one of his first stories — and perhaps for his later desire to discover the world. In this story, Ernest punished Grace by having his hero declare that his mother was dead; in works ranging from this childhood account to "Soldier's Home" and "The Mother of a Queen," he would go on evoking and exorcising the memories of his mother.

Ernest's relationship with his mother was therefore a complex and violent one that some see as the source of his turbulent, tortured relationships with the women in his life. His old friend Charles T. Lanham, who would later accompany him on the military campaign in Europe during the Second World War — from the June 1944 landings to the Ardennes Offensive — would say that he referred to her only as "that bitch." However, it was to her that in 1912 he dedicated the first poem of his that has been preserved. The woman who would always be "the dark queen of Hemingway's inner world" felt, for her part, devoted love for him. Affectionate letters and cakes — from someone who barely set foot in the kitchen — were offered in an attempt to win over and keep close, at least emotionally, this son who sought to escape her clutches. Even when he did not speak about her in such degrading terms, Ernest would give her anti-Semitic nicknames such as "Mrs. Hemingstein" or, shorter and with a nod to destiny, "Mrs. Stein."

1. 1907. The Hemingway children lined up on Memorial Day, in commemoration of war veterans. Grandfather Anson sports his uniform and Civil War medals, and Ernest (third left) a large pistol.

2. Ernest, a serious little man, posing with his parents and sisters, 1909.

3. Aged nine, Ernest writes to his father in a still-faltering hand: "On Sat. Mama and I went over the ford at the river. It is very much higher. I got six clames [clams] and some weat [weeds] six feet tall. Your loving son, Ernest M. Hemingway."

4. The Doctor and the doctor's Wife: Clarence and Grace, Ernest's parents, a year after their marriage, in 1897.

5. Ernest and Grace leaving for Nantucket, 1910.

1. The "twins" Ernest and Marcelline, brother and sister dressed as little girls, 1902.

2. Marcelline in the little boat bearing her name, at Windemere. Ursula also had her own small boat.

3. Clarence Hemingway crossing over a natural arch, a perfect example of magnificent American scenery.

Ernest was 18 months younger than his sister Marcelline, yet despite the difference in age and sex, for several years Grace Hemingway insisted on raising Ernest and Marcelline as twins, going as far as dressing them both as girls and getting them to adopt similar behavior and routines. At the same time, Grace, who had named her son Ernest Miller in homage to her father and her brother, liked to highlight her child's masculinity, as demonstrated by the family photo albums in which she writes "my precious boy, a 'real' boy." Ernest, who proudly declared to all and sundry that he feared nothing, nonetheless confided one day to his mother that he was afraid that Santa Claus wouldn't know what to bring him because he wore the same clothes as his sister: how would he realize he was a boy? Ernest's lack of self-confidence and shyness perhaps date from this period, as well, perhaps, as the insomnia that would haunt him all his life. Although he would later attribute his anxieties to post-traumatic shock after the war, Scott Fitzgerald observed in the 1920s that they were certainly linked to his childhood. But what is most revealing is the fact that Ernest, who wrote about every period of his life and often very frankly, always remained inhibited about the relationship with his mother, as if he remained, in that regard, vulnerable.

Ernest's father was the man of the family. An obstetrician and passionate about fishing and hunting, he had an intimate knowledge of the woods and swamps of northern Michigan as well as of its American Indian populations. He was an austere man with rigid notions of morality: naturally, he did not tolerate cigarettes or alcohol but also condemned cards and, like a good Puritan, dancing. When Grace took her "twins" to dancing classes and, the height of immorality, organized an afternoon dance in their honor at their new residence on North Kenilworth Avenue, Clarence felt that he had abdicated his role as head of the family in favor of his wife. Ernest would portray this couple, whose relationship seems full of repressed tension, in "The Doctor and the Doctor's Wife" and other stories, notably "Fathers and Sons," in which the father lists a series of "abominable crimes," all sexual in nature. In the words of his character Nick, his father "was as sound [on hunting and fishing] as he was unsound on sex." Clarence took his son along on his expeditions through the wooded, largely uncivilized regions of northern Michigan and impressed Ernest with his aptitude for weapons and his eagle-eyed vision — Ernest's sight was already weakening.

Clarence and Grace Hemingway with their daughters Marcelline and Ursula, sitting on a "worm fence," the typical Midwest enclosure celebrated by the poet Walt Whitman.

1. Windemere, the Hemingways' summer residence in northern Michigan.

2. Clarence, champion fisher and hunter, taught Ernest these skills.

3. Interior of the summer residence; Grace composed a hymn of praise to it here: "Lovely Walloona."

Opposite page: 1916. In nature, Ernest composes some of his first writings.

In 1900, the family acquired a summer home on the banks of Walloon Lake as a haven from the inland summer heat. The residence was called Windemere, a name chosen by Ernest's mother in reference to the English lake and Oscar Wilde's famous literary character (although the first R of the lake and of Lady Windermere would rapidly disappear). The region, still densely populated by Ojibway, would be another training ground for the young Ernest, who fished and hunted there with his father but also alone or in the company of the loyal friends who would later people the stories featuring Nick Adams. His first letters to his father from Paris, some 20 years later, would still bear the traces of this early apprenticeship; in them he gave detailed descriptions of newly discovered species in the Luxembourg gardens or the Jardin d'acclimatation. The world of nature into which his father had initiated him would never be far for Ernest, even when he lived in cities like Paris, New York or Madrid. His excursions into the great outdoors would inform so many forays into the world of writing, providing metaphors for the discovery of life, sexuality and death, as in "Big Two-Hearted River." Ernest developed his keen sense of observation and began to write notes and poems inspired by his reflections. In the final years of his American childhood, his first writings would also be published in his high school newspaper and yearbook.

A String of 63 fish.

Before Breakfast - Aug. 1861.

She & me come up from the bath. Dripping but triumphant. Summer of 1901

"**WINDEMERE**"

WALLOON LAKE, MICH.

Ernest Miller Hemingway's blond curls cut off at Windemere when he was 2 yrs 1 mo old

Aug. 1901.

Family album. Clarence, Marcelline and Ernest at Windemere, in 1901.

his passionate interest in nature would give him a taste for independence and for self-transcendence as well as a certain physical toughness. These values were profoundly anchored in the American Protestant ethic that had been made fashionable again by the 26th president of the United States, Theodore Roosevelt, hero and guiding figurehead of the nation. Ernest's rough individualism, bred by hunter-gatherer activities on the shores of Lake Michigan, was now augmented by a national, even nationalistic, pride embodied by the figure of Roosevelt. The latter was at the origin not only of the popularization of the image of the "cowboy" — who had undergone a transformation from basic cowherd to icon — but also the creation of an American spirit composed of Protestant values, confrontation with nature and a sense of national identity. It was with this sentiment of belonging to both Christianity and America that Ernest, dressed in the khaki that was Roosevelt's distinguishing characteristic and that would become his own, went in 1909 to cheer on the president when his hero of the moment passed through Oak Park.

It was also in 1909, on the occasion of his 10th birthday, that his father gave him his first rifle, with which he posed proudly. Weapons would feature all through Ernest's life: veritable talismans that affirmed masculinity and that constituted one of the linking themes that were passed down through the generations of Hemingways.

For many years, Ernest enjoyed a privileged relationship with his father, who represented a focus of stability for him; it was "a relief to them both to escape into a man's world, without women." Like most other adolescents, however, as he grew older he would move away from the hero worship of his childhood. All the more markedly in Ernest's case because of his refusal to accept what he saw as Clarence's subjugation to Grace. The fatal blow to his admiration for his father came in 1912, when Clarence took rest cures for his nerves. Stories like "My Old Man" or late novels like *Islands in the Stream* retrace this apocalyptic time in which the simultaneous cruelty and weakness of fathers is revealed.

1. Ernest and one of his first hunting trophies, around 1913.

2. Theodore Roosevelt at the head of his cavalry regiment during the taking of San Juan Hill, the American-Spanish war, 1898.

3. Roosevelt and "his" elephant, during his safari of 1909.

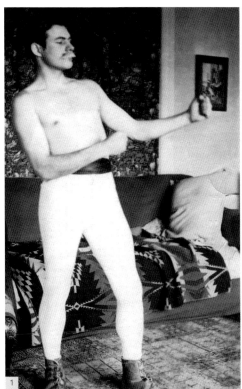

n 1911, the Hemingways' fifth child was born — another sister, Carol — and then finally, in 1915, Ernest's only brother, Leicester Clarence. Ernest's American childhood was coming to an end; he was 16 and soon to leave high school. In the meantime, like all educated boys of his age, he studied algebra, Latin, English and science. An accomplished sportsman, he belonged to the varsity sports team at school and wore their pullover with pride. Football and swimming — in which he excelled — formed part of his physical education. Ernest liked scrapping, and, cheered on by his sisters, he would exchange blows in front of the family house and then, when the fights got too brutal, in more discreet venues. For Ernest did not just like to box: he liked to win. "The sweet smile on his face masked the savagery in his heart," and many playmates became adversaries to be beaten. If it is not certain that he took boxing lessons in Chicago, as he would later claim, he did see some important fights there. Boxing and fisticuffs would remain markedly important to him, and life as combat was a metaphor central to his work.

1. Ernest posing as a boxer in the manner of John L. Sullivan. Chicago, 1921.

2. Grace and her children Leicester (the baby of the family), Carol, Madelaine, Ursula, Ernest and Marcelline. Windemere, 1916.

3. Ernest posing with his high school football team, November 1915.

As he was emerging from adolescence, real combat approached Ernest's life. On April 6, 1917, when men had already been massacring each other in the bloody trenches of Europe for three years, the United States entered the war. On June 13, Ernest finished his school career. He was reading an autobiographical war novel by the English writer Hugh Walpole (another of whose books, *Fortitude*, he would mention in "The End of Something"). This novel, *The Dark Forest*, constitutes one of Ernest's strange, disturbing connections between biography and fiction. Walpole writes in a Victorian style from which Ernest would distance himself, but the basic outline of the novel could have been one of his own: a young man rejected by the army because of his poor eyesight volunteers for the Red Cross then falls madly in love with a young nurse in a defining experience of love and death[1]. One recognizes, at one and the same time, both the intrigue of Ernest's life and that of his second great novel, *A Farewell to Arms*. For the moment, however, Ernest saw arms only in his imagination. His father refused to let him join up and insisted he go with his sister Marcelline to study at Oberlin, in the family tradition. Ernest refused. Wearying of the argument, his father eventually got him a place, through his brother, on the *Kansas City Star*, where Ernest would be a freelance cub reporter.

The young man, thirsty for action, very soon tired of reporting on humdrum municipal affairs. He eventually managed to get himself sent into Kansas City's police stations and hospital to investigate small local matters and accidents. This suited him better. Under the iron rule of his editor, he began to develop the style that would become his own and that bore the mark of his journalistic beginnings: short, hard-hitting, concise sentences from which adjectives were banned. As Aaron Hotchner would later report, Ernest began to distrust "big words." The capital of Missouri, Kansas City, was the nerve center of jazz in the 1920s, and a feverishness, not to say a certain violence, reigned over the city. If Ernest did not change radically during his time there, he nonetheless experienced a taste of freedom and independence and also, for the first time, an environment in which the moral and sexual codes and customs of Oak Park were challenged.

Opposite page, 1, 2, 3: Life in the woods, 1916. His peregrinations, here with, among others his faithful friend Lewis Clarahan, were precious to the young Ernest.

4, 5. Ernest posing for the camera on a freight train, in the manner of vagabonds who used these trains as a means of transport, 1898.

To Ernest, however, it was clear that Missouri was only a stepping stone and that he would join up with the American forces. A letter of 1942 shows the naivety of the young man he then was: "I was an awful dope ... I can remember thinking that we were the home team and the Austrians the visiting team." Although he always said that his weak eyesight prevented him from joining the regular army, it is likely that the combination of novelistic impressions created in him by *The Dark Forest* and a certain realism had, "for all his patriotism," put Ernest off "the prospect of trench warfare." Instead, he signed up, along with a friend, as a volunteer ambulance driver for the American Red Cross, received the handsome uniform of a second lieutenant and paraded down Fifth Avenue in view of President Woodrow Wilson before setting sail on May 21, 1917, to cross an Atlantic Ocean swarming with German U-boats. His story "Night Before Landing" would evoke that crossing in which he left America for the first time — as well as his childhood and an unfinished novel that would never be resumed, "Along with Youth." Several weeks before his departure, he went on a last fishing and canoeing expedition with friends who would stay behind, a trip that would later be evoked in "Indian Camp," in which the young Nick dangles his hand in the cold water of the river and "felt quite sure he would never die."

Opposite page: Ernest fishing in the water, like Nick in "Big Two-Hearted River," around 1916. There is as much thoughtfulness in the gesture as there is in the composition of the picture.

Left: Proud of his trout, in a pose that would become familiar. Horton Bay, around 1919.

IN ANOTHER COUNTRY

Hemingway's European Education

"In the fall the war was always there, but we did not go to it any more." Thus opens "In Another Country," one of Ernest's most moving stories about war, a story that he would always class as one of his favorites. Characteristically, although the war was raging everywhere, it was absent from this tale that recounted the quiet, stoic despair of wounded veterans in a hospital in Milan, far from the front. Biographies of Hemingway all agree that he was always acutely sensitive to a sense of place and his "geographical descriptions were indeed painfully conscious." The title and the opening of the story suggest that for Ernest the war was not so much a historical event as a strange and painful terrain; with the physical and emotional wounds it causes, it would always form part of his life, even when it was described only implicitly or else as a lack or an absence. Ernest would declare in 1958 that he had always wanted to be a writer, yet it was only on his return from the front during the first war in which he took part that his literary life really began. Of course, his formal education had taken place at school in Oak Park and then as a cub reporter on the *Kansas City Star*, and he had even published several short pieces in local magazines, but it was the war that would constitute, in the sense meant by Romain Gary in his book of the same name, Hemingway's European education and his full entry into the world of writing.

Ernest would live through more than half of the 20th century and take part in three of its wars. In 1951, when he was in Havana, he confided that he felt "black ass" (depressed) because of Korea: "This is the first time my country ever fought that I was not there, and food has no taste, and the hell with love when you can't have children." This remark illustrates how love and death, life and war, were always entwined for Ernest. Stories and three novels, the great classics *A Farewell to Arms*, *For Whom the Bell Tolls* and then later the poorly received *Across the River and Into the Trees*, all bore traces of his military experiences. Yet these works transcend biography, for if "the geography is perfectly accurate," Ernest was unable to have direct experience of war before writing about it. On his brief foray into the Austro-Italian front, he did not experience combat like Frederick Henry, the hero of *A Farewell to Arms*, yet so immediate and authentic is his description of the Italian retreat from Caporetto in the third part of the novel that critics found it hard to believe that Ernest had not taken part in it.

Opposite page, 1, 2: His passport photos, 1921.

3. The appeal of the open sea. Here, Ernest is 15. Three years later he would undertake his first big journey, to Europe and the war.

On his arrival in Europe in the spring of 1918, Ernest went through Bordeaux and then Paris, which was under fire from German artillery. At the beginning of June he was in Milan, where the first task given the 18-year-old boy was that of gathering up pieces of bodies scattered throughout the landscape after a munitions factory had blown up. The narrator of "The Natural History of the Dead" notes, in a tone of controlled despair, that "one becomes so accustomed to the sight of all the dead being men that the sight of a dead woman is quite shocking." Death, given and received, acquired a gender and a face; this was no longer death in its abstract, triumphal or heroic guise. Hemingway also expressed surprise at seeing "the human body blown into pieces which exploded along no anatomical lines." War interrupts and dislocates the grammar of the body. In fiction, this grammar is restored to mutilated lives through its depiction of the reality of war.

Stationed behind the lines for a time, near Milan, Ernest was a little too far from the heat of the action for his liking. Much later, upon making friends with the famous American writer John Dos Passos, he learned that they would certainly have crossed each others' paths at that time; in 1918, however, the two men barely paid any attention to each other. Ernest was bored. He wrote to Ted Brumback, the friend with whom he had joined up: "I am going to get out of this ambulance section and see if I can't find where the war is."

1. Soldier Hemingway in uniform, 1918.

2. At the wheel of his ambulance, the Italian front.

3. Firing squad, Italian front, 1918.

1. An ambulance, similar to Ernest's, goes behind the lines.

2. View of the front. The inscription on the wall reads "Better to live a day as a lion than a century as a sheep."

3, 4. Looking war and death in the face.

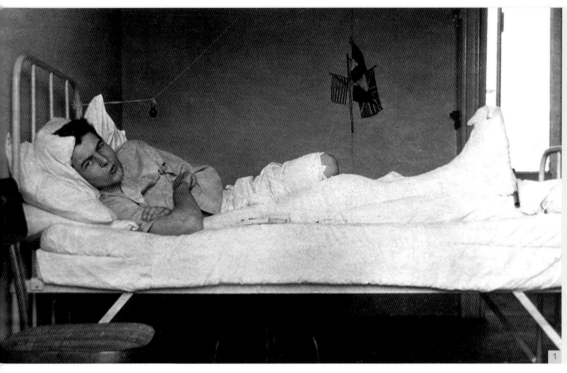

But it was the war that would find him. Around July 6, his unit was transferred to Schio, in the outer foothills of the Dolomites, and on the 8th, after he had decided to distribute chocolate and cigarettes to keep up the troops' morale, he was hit by shrapnel. These bursts of shellfire were designed to mutilate and thereby drive a man, a nation and even a whole generation to despair. Ernest would describe these mutilations almost obsessively in practically all his books. Jake Barnes in *The Sun Also Rises* would lose his virility in the war under the "Hun theory that nothing takes a soldier out faster than to have his balls shot off." Also mutilated were Nick in "Cross-Country Snow," the new father in "Indian Camp," Harry Morgan in *To Have and Have Not* and many others. In the meantime, some 200 pieces ("227," he specified) of shrapnel were removed from Ernest's leg. He would keep some of them in a small wallet that never left him. If his first letters to his family were reassuring, proclaiming that he would be up in two weeks, his wound was serious and required a long convalescence at the Ospedale Croce Rossa Americana in Milan. Ernest Hemingway would never again go to the front.

Soon afterward he was nominated for the Silver Medal for Valor. He had been in the background; now here he was promoted to the rank of hero. Like tens of thousands of men, Ernest was wounded, as he put it in *A Farewell to Arms*, "in a flash, as when a blast-furnace door is swung open." There are contradictory and differing accounts of what really happened that July 8, Ernest having embroidered and exaggerated the facts. The most authentic version is undoubtedly that depicted in *A Farewell to Arms* and stories like "Now I Lay Me" and "A Very Short Story."

Repatriated to the United States at the beginning of 1919, his ship landed on January 21 and the *New York Sun* devoted an article to him. In his native town, he gave an interview to the *Oak Parker*, in which he gave a singularly exaggerated account of his exploits. It may have been just

1. Ernest on his sickbed at the Red Cross hospital, July 1918.

2. Convalescent, but his leg still stiff, September 1918.

3, 4. Convalescence in Milan.

5. Gathering in honor of the hero Hemingway on his return home, February 16, 1919.

6. Ernest's medal for bravery.

to "have some fun at the expense of gullible civilians," but the fact remains that he related war stories that associated him with the Italian *partigiani* (resistance fighters) and launched the myth that he had been wounded in machine-gun crossfire — with 28 bullets being removed from his body, without anesthetic. Ernest was starting to construct his personality, as well as a reputation as a shameless braggart. Later, as a war correspondent in the Spanish Civil War, he would claim to have taken part in the fighting on the Republican side, adding for good measure that in the heat of battle he had had to urinate on a machine gun to unjam it. After the 1944 American invasion of France, he said that he had "liberated" the Ritz in Paris, but again this is part of the Hemingway legend that Ernest himself and several of his adoring admirers would perpetuate. It is true that on that day, in defiance of the Geneva convention, Ernest flaunted his status as war correspondent to join the fighting, even going so far as to lead a small band of resistance fighters. The photographer Robert Capa thought Hemingway must be, at the very least, a three-star general, so luxurious was his lifestyle with his chauffeur, his personal assistant, his impressive arsenal and his stock of supplies, in which there was no shortage of wine and cognac. His character Colonel Cantwell would declare in *Across the River* that "[t]he taking of Paris was nothing, ... only an emotional experience," but it was on that occasion that Ernest saw the war at closer hand. When the authorities later asked him to explain his irregular activities under oath, he denied everything point-blank and even embellished further to make himself look good. To his biographers he would serve up an official version of events according to which his companions-in-arms were "sick," which allegation tarnished their friendship. C.T. "Buck" Lanham, in particular, would say that Ernest had recounted nonsense to inflate his importance and concluded that he was "magnificent in the war but insufferable in peace."

Numero d'ordine del Registro delle concessioni 27458

Regio Esercito Italiano

Il Comandante del V Corpo d'Armata

Visto il R. Decreto 19 Gennaio 1918. n. 205.

Determina:

È concessa al Volontario *Hemingway M. Ernest*

di Ernst da Oak Park - C. R. Americana - 4° Sez.ne Autoambulanza

la Croce al Merito di Guerra

Zona di Guerra, addì 18 Dicembre 1918

Il Tenente Generale
Comandante del Corpo d'Armata

Order of Merit certificate in the name of the young ambulance driver Hemingway, Italy, 1918.

THE OAK PARKER

Published every Saturday at 723 Lake
street, Oak Park, Ill., by
THE OAK PARKER COMPANY
Phones: Oak Park 7800, 7801, 7802

ALBERT E. BERRY..............President
M. A. J. BERRY..........Secretary-Treasurer

Entered as second class matter at the Oak Park,
Ill. Postoffice.

Subscription rate $2.00 per year, payable in
advance
Advertising rates upon application

FIRST LIEUTENANT HEMINGWAY

Comes Back Riddled With Bullets and Decorated With Two Medals

By Roselle Dean

When the war broke out Ernest M. Hemingway was wielding a pencil for the Kansas City Star. His future looked promising as a newspaper man, for Ernest had a style of diction that was all his own. When uniforms began to collect and circulate about the streets, the young scribe lost his interest in "scoops" and "spreads" and waxed moody and restless. The spirit of the war was in his veins! One day he tossed the pencil into the waste basket and started out to enlist. But here his patriotic spirit met with rebuff—for one of Ernest's bright brown eyes did not work as nimbly as it should in the estimation of the navy and Marine Corps recruiting inspectors. Even the British army could not overlook that eye—which to all appearances, is a perfectly good orb. But Ernest had the patriotic spirit and enthusiasm of nineteen years, and he made up his mind to "go over" at all costs. Then his opportunity came to get into the Italian ambulance service, and the young scribe sailed across—with the eye that had caused him so much trouble in enlisting—and had no doubt to its credit a record for breaking hearts. Last May he landed in the Trentino mountains of Italy and was in the big Austrian offensive along the Piave river. He moved later to Fossalta and became attached to an Italian infantry regiment there, remaining from the middle of June until he was wounded on the 8th of July. In the fight at Fossalta he was wounded three times when he went with a motor truck into the front lines to distribute cigarets and block chocolate to the soldiers. In No Man's Land, he was at the observation post when a big shell came in and burst, hitting him and killing two Italian soldiers at his side. This felled the young hero, deeply implanting shot in both knees. As soon as he was able to crawl, however, and still under fire, he picked up a wounded man and carried him on his back to the Italian trenches, despite the fact that he was knocked down twice by machine gun fire, which struck him in the left thigh and right foot. In all, Lieutenant Hemingway received thirty-two 45-caliber bullets in his limbs and hands, all of which have been removed, except one in the left limb which the young warrior is inclined to foster as a souvenir—if his surgeon-father does not deprive him of this novel keepsake.

In view of all the shot and shell which lodged itself in this soldier's body while he plunged without fear into the most dangerous places, his commission, the silver medal of valor and the cross of war are honors none too great for him to bring back. The greatest thing of

FIRST LIEUTENANT HEMINGWAY
Returns from the Ambulance Service
in Italy

all, perhaps not to him, for death could have had no terrors for one who persisted in facing it as he did, but to those who love him, was that he has lived to come back.

Lieutenant Hemingway scoffs at being referred to as "a hero." "I went because I wanted to go," he said, in his frank way. "I was big and strong, my country needed me, and I went and did whatever I was told—and anything I did outside of that was simply my duty." To interview this officer, something over six feet tall and handsome as an Apollo, was quite enervating, for, after having beguiled him into The Oak Parker office, he was not disposed to talk about himself. Only in a general phase of conversation were his views on the war gleaned. His valor, however, preceded him across seas—his medals and Italian newspapers tell the rest. On being pinned down, he did admit that encountering a bullet was like being hit with an icy snowball, the pain arriving some time later. Lieutenant Hemingway submitted to having twenty-eight bullets extracted without taking an anaesthetic. His only voluntary comment on the war is that it was "great sport" and he is ready to go "on the job" if it ever happens again.

No story is quite complete without a thread of romance, and we are inclined to believe that somewhere in sunny Italy there is a dark-eyed, olive-skinned beauty, whose heart beats for one—and one only—"Americano" soldier, who arrived in the U. S. on the Verdi about a week ago and is now domiciled with his parents, Mr. and Mrs. C. E. Hemingway, at 600 North Kenilworth avenue.

A soldier-grandfather, Anson T. Hemingway, at 400 North Oak Park avenue, who did his bit in the Civil War, also rises with the rest of us to salute "First Lieut. Ernest M. Hemingway, hero of the Italian war ambulance service."

FIRST PRESBYTERIAN NOTES

Dr. John M. Vander Muelen of the First Presbyterian church preached in Detroit last Sunday, occupying the pulpit of Dr. Joseph Vance, formerly pastor of the Hyde Park church of Chicago. In his absence the pulpit of the First Presbyterian church was filled morning and evening by Rev. John E. Kuizenga of Holland, Mich., a professor in the Western Theological seminary of the Reformed Church of America and a long-time friend of the Oak Park pastor.

Dr. Kuizenga is one of the strong men of the denomination and, unlike some other specialists in his profession, his work in the study and classroom has not diminished his power as a great preacher. His large audiences both morning and evening expressed their high appreciation of the man and his message.

Dr. Kuizenga selected as his theme for his evening serman "The Limitations of Life," based on Paul's words in "Remember my bonds." He said when Paul wrote these words he was chained to a Roman soldier, and this was his delicate apology for his signature to a letter which he had dictated to another person. Every life, he said, had its limitations either of birth, of race or of conditions. In the second place, God reckons with our limitations. At the end He will not ask, "How far did you get?" but "How far have you come?" Browning expresses this thought in the words, "All that I aspired to be, but failed to be, comforts me." In the third place, our limitations are our supreme opportunity. "This does not mean that we accept the doctrine of submissions as a sort of fatalism," said the preacher. "I know a girl who hated God because she was homely, and her mother had told her that she ought not to complain, for God had made her that way. But God overrules the limitations of life and makes even the afflictions and hard experiences to widen the spiritual horizon and minister to the freedom of the soul."

A solo by Mrs. Smith of the choir, beautifully sung, reinforced the appeal of the sermon.

Music at Second Presbyterian

Program of music to be given Sunday evening, February 2, at the Second Presbyterian Church by the quartet, composed of Mrs. Alfred Newman, soprano; Miss Anna C. Braun, contralto; Arthur Jones, tenor; Murray C. Eldredge, bass, and Miss Edna L. Whitmore, organist:

Prelude—Grand Offertoire in D.........Batiste
　　　　　Miss Whitmore
The Strain Upraise.................Buck
　　　　　Quartet
Watchman, What of the Night?........Sargent
　　Mr. Jones and Mr. Eldredge
Oh, For a Closer Walk With God.......Radcliff
　　　　　Quartet
The Voice in the Wilderness.............Scott
　　　　　Miss Braun
Sanctus . . ..Gounod
　　　　　Quartet
Postlude—March in B Flat...............Silas
　　　　　Miss Whitmore

The Edgar Rice Burroughs home at 325 North Oak Park avenue has been leased to W. W. Fowler, 426 Clinton avenue. The lease was made by G. Whittier Gale & Co.

The article about Ernest that appeared in the *Oak Parker* on his return to Illinois.

On his return from the front in 1919, Ernest's leg wound was healing well but he was suffering from what was not yet termed post-traumatic stress. He was assaulted by insomnia and the first episodes of depression; he fought them with reading, drives into the countryside and, already, alcohol. In Milan, he had fallen seriously in love for the first time; Ernest's life always imitating fiction, the beloved was a nurse — reminiscent of Walpole's *The Dark Forest*. She was older than he was and her name was Agnes von Kurowsky. The real-life story did not have a happy ending, Agnes leaving Ernest to set her sights on an Italian officer, but she would be sublimated through the character of Catherine Barkley in *A Farewell to Arms* — the detour into reality having been a short one.

Although he might have left that strange country of war for a time, Ernest took from it what was his most precious and inspiring material: wounds of body and soul, confrontation with death, a sense of abandonment, even betrayal, the conviction that he would always be a man without a woman — themes that would inhabit the fiction of his life and the life of his fiction.

1. Ernest flirting with Agnes von Kurowsky.

2. Walking with Agnes and chaperones. This scene would appear in *A Farewell to Arms*.

t was not long before Ernest found war again. In September 1922, he was sent by the *Toronto Star* to cover the Greek retreat from Thrace and the exodus of a population during what was the first ethnic cleansing of the century. The confusion of the conflict and its absurd violence appeared in the cynical, disillusioned tone of "On the Quai at Smyrna," a tone he would recapture in *Death in the Afternoon*. In the latter he depicts the mothers who refused to have their dead babies taken from them and the mules thrown into the water with broken forelegs and left to cry out in agony for days. This hell "called for a Goya" to depict the Horrors of War, says the narrator of *Death in the Afternoon*, but immediately adds in a touch of black humor by suggesting that if these dying animals had been capable of demanding anything, they would in all likelihood not "call for pictorial representation in their plight but ... call for someone to alleviate their condition." This stoicism and the brutal detachment that went with it constituted Ernest's attitude to war. The physical and emotional wounding had shattered the sense of heroic, grandiose combat. It is again this cynicism that we find with Jake Barnes, protagonist and antihero of *The Sun Also Rises*. Contemplating his emasculated body in the mirror, Jake says: "Of all the ways to be wounded. I suppose it was funny." War holds out a mirror to men, showing them both their grandeur and their ignominy, conferring on them the mask of undamaged virility.

Even if Ernest understands, like his protagonists, the inanity of war, he is nonetheless fascinated by it, pursuing and wooing it and seeing it as the "greatest of outdoor sports." For him, it was a test of his courage and masculinity, a display of self — in both an existential and a narcissistic sense — that he would seek out as war reporter, aficionado of bullfighting or big-game hunter. He liked to get close to danger and over time would develop a stoicism worthy of his heroes: "having conquered his fears, he took a hard line towards those who could not cast off their own." *For Whom the Bell Tolls* denounces *cobardes*, cowards who did not know how to look life and death in the face. Among them was Ernest's father, who had shot himself in the head in 1928. It would take his son 10 years to be able to write about this death, in the character of Robert Jordan, who offers a sombre reflection on the memories of a grandfather fighting in the Indian wars, the cowardice of a father who committed suicide and a mother, "that woman," an absent figure who, in Ernest's own words, would send him for Christmas the revolver with which his father had killed himself, telling him it would be good if he kept it. Jordan is heartbroken by his father's deed: "[H]e was a *cobarde*. Go on, say it in English. Coward. ... He was just a coward and that was the worst luck any man could have." As far as Ernest was concerned, you either had balls or you didn't.

March 7, 1919

Jan 22. 1922

Dear Kid:-

Well, when your voice from the past reached me, after I recovered from the surprise, I never was more pleased over anything in my life. I know there has always been a little bitterness over the way our courtship ended, especially since I got back & Mrs. read me the very bitter letter you wrote her about me. (He means that she had already read it to "the Doc"— whom you may recall hearing in those dim days.)

Anyhow, I always knew that it would turn out right in the end, & that you would realize it was the best way, as I'm positive you must believe now that you have Hadley. Think of what an antique I am at the present writing, and my ghost should simply burst on the spot, leaving only a little smoke that will evaporate.

Oh, gosh — there's so much to tell you. I ... leaving ... was ruined for America, & when the poor Doc much faster, ambled around I was as nasty as possible, tho' he stuck fast until I sailed the 2nd time, when he promptly married, & now is struggling along & has a young son.

I worked in Miss Shaw's Tuberculosis Social Service Department for 6 months, & then went home for a visit, and came back to N.Y. just when things were beginning to stir up again in Europe. So I was slated for Russia & sailed in March 1920. I didn't tell my friends & relatives it was to be Russia, as they all had an idea it was certain death, as a suspected spy & venture over the borders of that poor land. But dern it all, when I got to Paris, Russia was closed, especially for women workers, & I went to Bucharest with 2 other

Ernie, dear boy,

I am writing this late at night after a long think by myself, & I am afraid it is going to hurt you, but, I'm sure it won't harm you permanently.

For quite awhile before you left, I was trying to convince myself it was a real love-affair, because, we always seemed to disagree, & then arguments always wore me out so that I finally gave in to keep you from doing something desperate.

Now, after a couple of months away from you, I know that I am still very fond of you, but, it is more as a mother than as a sweetheart. It's alright to say I'm a Kid, but, I'm not, & I'm getting less & less so every day.

So, Kid (still Kid to me, & always will be) can you forgive me some day for unwittingly deceiving you? You know I'm not really bad, & don't mean to do wrong, & now I realize it was my fault in the beginning that you cared for me, & regret it from the bottom of my heart. But, I am now & always will be too old, & that's the truth, & I can't get away from the fact that you're just a boy — a kid.

I somehow feel that some day I'll have reason to be proud of you, but, dear boy, I can't wait for that day, & it was wrong to hurry a career.

I tried hard to make you understand a bit of what I was thinking on that trip from Padua to Milan, but, you acted like a spoiled child, & I couldn't keep on hurting you. Now, I only have the courage because I'm far away.

Then — & believe me when I say this is sudden for me, too — I expect to be married soon. And I hope & pray that after you thought things out, you'll be able to forgive me & start a wonderful career & show what a man you really are.

Ever admiringly & fondly,

Your friend,
Aggie

Although he had become a successful author who could have taken things easy, with Hollywood making film adaptations (to his ever-greater displeasure) of his books and his discovery of new territory, principally Africa, Ernest took to the battlefields again, this time in Spain. A fierce lover of the country, he staunchly opposed the Spanish Army's *Pronunciamiento* of 1936, and with the considerable income generated by "The Snows of Kilimanjaro," "The Short Happy Life of Francis Macomber" and *To Have and Have Not*, he paid for two American volunteers to travel to Spain to fight in the Republican cause and contributed to the purchase of two ambulances. From Wyoming, where he had spent the summer in the company of his second wife, Pauline, he wrote to his editor Max Perkins at the publisher Scribner's, "I hope to go to Spain if it isn't all over."

Later he would temper his impatience to have a go at Franco, whom he roundly denounced, at the head of a "Hemingstein division," but events speeded up when in a Key West bar he met a journalist who had come to interview him. Love and war were again about to combine in his life. Martha Gellhorn was 30 years old: a very talented, very blonde, very beautiful journalist. Pauline, for whom Ernest had left Hadley, realized that history was about to repeat itself.

From January 1937, he was in Madrid, where he rubbed shoulders with some of the best representatives of modernism and antifascism, including André Malraux, Pablo Neruda and Antoine de Saint-Exupéry. He had a contract with the North American Newspaper Association to cover the conflict. He and John Dos Passos set up a company to produce documentaries to indoctrinate the American public about the Republican cause, which would include the film *The Spanish Earth* by the Dutch communist director Joris Ivens.

Opposite page: Spain, 1937.

1. Ernest (third left) on the front of the Spanish war; the director Joris Ivens is standing extreme right.

2. Martha, smiling and courageous, around 1937.

Ernest took part in political meetings, notably at Gaylord's Hotel, and these would become material for *For Whom the Bell Tolls*, his great lyrical hymn to the war. In the book, it is during a meeting in this hotel that Karkov, the Republicans' Bolshevik strategist, gives the naive American Robert Jordan a lesson in Marxism and realpolitik. Jordan, nicknamed el Inglés, a professor of Spanish literature who had come from America to test his courage and his idealism, is told by his political mentor: "[Y]ou have not been a professor now for almost nine months. In nine months you may have learned another trade." These nine months have indeed given birth to a new man, a man fashioned by war, a man who had received, in Gary's words, "that famous European education that teaches you ... how to find the courage and the right reasons, very valid, very correct reasons, to kill a man who has never done anything to you." "Do you think you have a right to kill?" Robert Jordan thus asks himself. War is this place in which beliefs and perceptions are tested and which Ernest would seek all his life to explore.

In Paris, Ernest had said to Ivens: "My beautiful girlfriend is coming. She has legs that begin at her shoulders." At Gaylord's, in a Madrid under siege of bombs, his affair with Martha (who had followed him to Spain on her own account as a journalist) took on public notoriety. In 1939, after several trips back and forth between the United States and Spain, he launched into writing *For Whom the Bell Tolls*, which is dedicated to Martha. Before that, in November 1938, he had made a last trip to Spain before the dictatorship. During the conflict he demonstrated a disarming political angelism that burst out in differences of view or even quarrels with other engaged intellectuals like Dos Passos. More a fascinated spectator of the war than an active participant in it, he would have neither the idealist vision of a Malraux and his *L'Espoir* (Man's Hope) or the commitment of an Orwell and his *Homage to Catalonia*. War, for Ernest, was a territory that allowed one to discover oneself and one's limits, both physical and existential. Without doubt he became "the victim of his own facile reporting and his novelist's self-absorption, which was heightened by his love affair with Martha." But Ernest was neither a historian nor a philosopher and, rather than a political or historical concept, war for him was primarily a vehicle for his writing.

"I only write once on any one theme; if I don't write it all in one time, it's not worth saying." Like the other topographies of his life, Ernest used, then abandoned the subjects of his work. The same went for war. Once he had explored it, the subject would be left behind him, in the manner of a farmer slashing and burning his fields or a hunter moving on to new territory after he had exhausted the old.

1. Ambulances similar to those Ernest sent from Cuba to the Spanish Republicans.

2. Spanish partisans read about the progress of the war in the newspaper.

3. Valencia, December 1937, by Robert Capa. Ernest writes between bombardments.

4. Contemplating death after an attack.

5, 6. Daily life as seen by Ernest during the Spanish Civil War, with its little markets and streams of refugees.

7. Teruel, December 1937, by Robert Capa. Leading the rough life of the front.

1. Teruel, December 1937. The photographer Robert Capa captures an Ernest marked by the horrors of war.

2. The Spanish pueblos, victims of the bombardments but also of the fratricidal war between villagers.

3. In Teruel, December 1937, by Robert Capa. Ernest was becoming a recognizable face of the war.

4. 1937. Civilians during the Spanish Civil War, of which Ernest would draw a moving portrait in *For Whom the Bell Tolls*; Joris Ivens would do the same in the film *The Spanish Earth*, which Ernest would narrate.

5. Ernest and Martha on the front with Robert Merriman, commander of the Abraham Lincoln Brigade, composed of American antifascist volunteers.

1. Ernest and Martha en route for China, 1941.

2. A photographer immortalizing Ernest, who became as interesting a subject as the war itself.

3. Studying the map of the front with a Chinese officer, 1941.

4. Ernest lends his expert eye to the training of a soldier in Hankow.

5, 6. Ernest and Martha with Chinese officers, 1941.

Following double-page:
Paris, 1944.

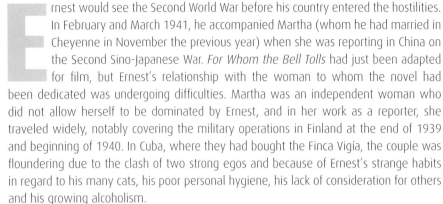

Ernest would see the Second World War before his country entered the hostilities. In February and March 1941, he accompanied Martha (whom he had married in Cheyenne in November the previous year) when she was reporting in China on the Second Sino-Japanese War. *For Whom the Bell Tolls* had just been adapted for film, but Ernest's relationship with the woman to whom the novel had been dedicated was undergoing difficulties. Martha was an independent woman who did not allow herself to be dominated by Ernest, and in her work as a reporter, she traveled widely, notably covering the military operations in Finland at the end of 1939 and beginning of 1940. In Cuba, where they had bought the Finca Vigía, the couple was floundering due to the clash of two strong egos and because of Ernest's strange habits in regard to his many cats, his poor personal hygiene, his lack of consideration for others and his growing alcoholism.

The war seemed to offer an escape route, but Ernest complained bitterly that Martha's "idea of fun ... was a honeymoon on the Burma Road." Martha was writing for *Collier's* and Ernest had managed to get an assignment for *PM*, a political news magazine. An exhausting journey by boat, plane, truck, foot, horse and car over some 30,000 miles (50,000 km) ensued. He sent only seven short dispatches in the course of this mammoth venture, during which Ernest barely saw the war, although through Joris Ivens he would meet Chu En-Lai and cautiously remark that Japan might well declare war on the United States. If this oriental detour constituted a welcome break for the Hemingways' rocky marriage, the trip itself was a big disappointment. Whether because China was the literary territory of André Malraux or because he felt he did not understand the country well enough, neither Ernest's emotions nor his intelligence were excited by the Sino-Japanese War and no work of fiction sprang from it.

Before the United States entered the war in December 1941, the Hemingways had returned to Cuba, where Ernest launched himself into extraordinary espionage and counterespionage activities, first on behalf of the FBI and then by equipping his fishing boat the *Pilar* to carry out antisubmarine patrols. Although Ernest managed to convince the authorities to engage him, on the basis of supposed observations of German U-boats off the Cuban coast, the *Pilar* never encountered the enemy. On the other hand, the special equipping of the boat meant that it was not subject to fuel rationing and could carry on catching swordfish undisturbed. As so often, Ernest's war became real only through fiction. On this occasion, it was the exploits of Gabriele d'Annunzio during the First World War and the spy novels of Graham Greene that would serve as a backdrop to Ernest's imagination. If the reports issued by the "Crook Factory," his spying organization, were "based more on fantasy than on fact" and would lead to its being shut down in 1943, the authorities nonetheless believed that Ernest's information and involvement would be valuable if German submarines approached the American coastline. It was only in 1944, when the navy had succeeded in securing the national territory, that the patrols of Ernest and his cronies would cease altogether. Hemingway, once again, remained quite far from the fighting; even though he was not awarded the medal for which he was nominated for his activities off the Cuban coast, in 1947 he received the Bronze Star for his work as a war correspondent and would remain "one of the most decorated non-combatants in military history [of the United States]."

1. With the American Army in France, 1944.

2, 3. Scenes of the liberation of Paris, in which Ernest took part.

4. The light-firearms permit delivered to Ernest in August 1944.

5. Ernest's war correspondent card, dated May 1944.

Ernest spent seven months, from June to December 1944, on the European front as a correspondent for *Collier's*, during which time he ended the relationship with Martha (whose place he had taken as special envoy). He began seeing Mary Welsh, who became his fourth wife. He considered the war to be his own special territory and was jealous and critical of those, such as Irwin Shaw, who had the audacity to write successfully on the subject. He called the Second World War "a good war," in the sense that it gave him the opportunity to demonstrate courage and independence and to share satisfying moments of manly companionship. He was working on a grand trilogy on the theme of war but, apart from six short articles, his only novel would be *Across the River and Into the Trees*, the story of a soldier who was wounded and broken — just like Ernest's memory, self-esteem and even "spelling and syntax." He knew that his reputation alone was enough to grant him every privilege, and he did not even try to write seriously for *Collier's*: he wanted to keep the best pieces for his next book.

But his reputation also did him a disservice on occasion. The military authorities, for example, not wanting to risk losing such a precious icon of communication, made him observe the Normandy landing from a boat, while he was champing at the bit to go onto the beach — especially since Martha had managed to go ashore with the troops! He met one of his military heroes, C.T. "Buck" Lanham, with whom he shared the French campaign. Lanham knew Ernest's excesses but tolerated or even encouraged them; like others, he was fascinated by the aura that Ernest radiated. Ernest participated with him in the terrible battle of Hürtgenwald in which 24,000 Americans were killed, wounded or taken prisoner and got involved in the fighting on several occasions, notably using a machine gun to fend off an attack on Lanham's command post. It was also at this time (October 28) that his son Jack, who had jumped behind enemy lines, was captured; he would not be released until May 1945. Suffering from pneumonia, Ernest returned to Paris, where he spent a last night with Martha, who had meanwhile asked for a divorce — both Ernest's marriage and his Second World War had just come to an end. *Across the River* spoke of this "after man" after the fighting, who gave his last breath to his "true love, [his] last and only and true love." War and its fury are necessary but not sufficient for a Hemingway protagonist: real courage is the confrontation, with dignity and fortitude, of his status as fallen, defeated hero.

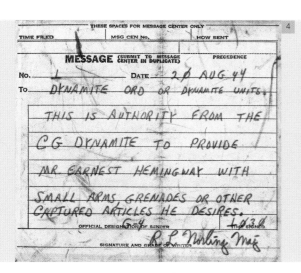

HE
MING-
WAY

A MOVEABLE FEAST

Paris, Song of Innocence and Experience

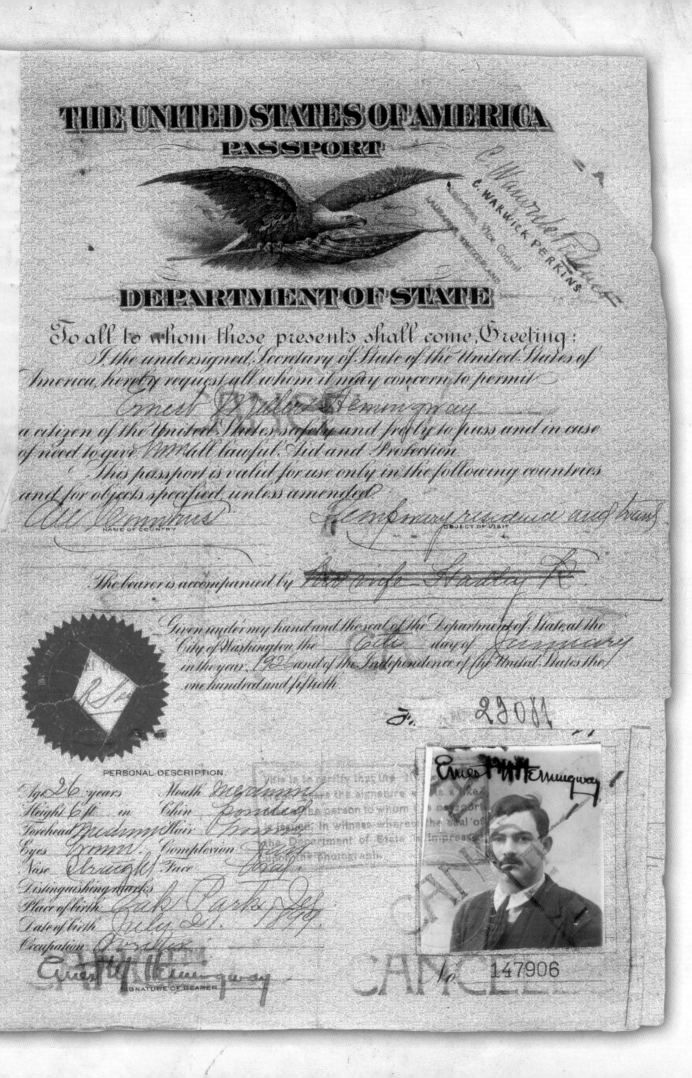

Paris, Song of Innocence and Experience

Ernest's life in Paris constituted only five years of his existence, between 1921 and 1925, yet it would become for him an indelible landscape, synonymous with happiness but also with destruction and disillusionment. Ernest arrived in Paris with his wife Hadley on December 20, 1921. A year earlier he had been dragging his boredom and malaise between Oak Park, Chicago and Canada, where he had begun to write for the *Toronto Star*. Several short stories also date from this time: "The Mercenaries," set in Sicily, which he visited after his operation in Milan, "The Current" and also "Crossroads: An Anthology." The magazines to which he sent the pieces all rejected them. Ernest began to doubt himself.

Things did not improve when his mother ordered him and his friend Ted Brumback, also home from the war, out of Windemere, the summer house where he had just celebrated his 21st birthday. At the same time, Grace handed him a letter in which she urged him to leave adolescence behind, writing that the world was crying out for "real men, with brawn and muscle, moral as well as physical — men whose mothers can look up to them instead of hanging their heads in shame at having borne them." In the puritanical Protestant tone that characterized her, she compared her maternal love to a bank account and concluded sharply that her son's was "overdrawn."

Ordered not to return to Windemere, Ernest and some friends went off into the wilds to fish and commune with nature like latter-day Robinson Crusoes, reading poems aloud around a campfire and dreaming of the Far East. However, these romantic dreams hid both the wound that his mother had inflicted on him and Ernest's real frustration at his uncertain future (he even thought about returning to Kansas City) and at finding himself without house or home. But the "summer's lease" of summer 1920 was as short as that of the preceding ones. It was time to make a decision. He wanted to head south with friends, but in the end he went north, to Chicago. There, toward the end of the year, he met a young woman with red hair named Hadley Richardson. After a brief courtship, he married her on September 3, 1921, in the small Methodist chapel of Walloon Bay near Oak Park. The families were in attendance — Ernest's doubtlessly delighted to see him taking the path of "real men." The honeymoon was spent at Windemere, and then the couple went to live, frugally (principally from Hadley's allowance), first in Chicago then Toronto. They began to discuss traveling to Europe.

Opposite page: Ernest's passport, 1925. In search of new horizons.

1. Joan Miró, *La Masia* (The Farm). Picture bought by Ernest for his first wife, Hadley; bequeathed by Mary Hemingway to the National Gallery of Art in Washington.

Below: wearing a beret, French-style, rue du Cardinal-Lemoine.

The American writer Sherwood Anderson explained to the aspiring young writer over dinner one evening that the best way to learn the craft of writing was to go to Paris. In addition, he pointed out that because of the favorable exchange rate, an American could live better in Paris than at home. Anderson offered to write letters of introduction for the young man and described, in the colorful style that characterized his prose, the human bestiary that he would encounter in this legendary Paris. His go-between would be a certain Lewis Galantière, who worked at the International Chamber of Commerce. Above all, however, he enjoined Ernest to embrace the Parisian elite of the arts and their fascination with modernism. He also must not fail to visit the peculiarly named Shakespeare and Company bookstore, run by a lady named Sylvia Beach. Anderson told him about writers whose future, he assured him, was brilliant: a curious Irishman by the name of James Joyce and Ezra Pound, a native of Idaho long since transplanted to Europe where his poetic force was beginning to be recognized. Not forgetting Gertrude Stein, a very remarkable lady who lived with the discreet Alice B. Toklas and who was a close friend of Picasso's and many other contemporary artists.

By the end of November, everything was prepared: Ernest would be the Paris correspondent of the *Toronto Star*, and the couple's crossing was reserved on the *Leopoldina* — "Maybe away from Paris I could write about Paris as in Paris I could write about Michigan," wrote Ernest in *A Moveable Feast*. Indeed, it was only in Cuba that he would talk about the French capital, but it was in Paris that an essential phase in his writing career occurred. As he would say later to Allan Hotchner, the fellow adventurer of the last 10 years of his life: "If you are lucky enough to have lived in Paris as a young man, then wherever you go for the rest of your life it stays with you, for Paris is a moveable feast."

1. Ezra Pound, around 1920.

2. Gertrude Stein with her portrait, painted by her protégé Picasso.

3. From left to right, John Dos Passos, Joris Ivens, Sidney Franklin and Hemingway, in Madrid.

Opposite page : Ernest and Sylvia Beach in front of Shakespeare and Company, a bookshop then situated at 12 rue de l'Odéon. The wound, one of the many he inflicted on himself in his life, was due to a ceiling he had brought down on his head by confusing the light cord with the toilet flusher. Paris, 1928.

Paris, Song of Innocence and Experience

Left page: Scene from the window of the kitchenette at 74 rue du Cardinal-Lemoine, around 1923.

1. Ernest in the courtyard of his building at 113 rue Notre-Dame-des-Champs. Paris, 1924.

2. Ernest was a knowledgeable racegoer who studied jockeys, horses and trainers. Racing remained a passion at every stage of his life.

As soon as he arrived, Ernest began sketching out his Parisian geography. The city was a new honeypot and exciting in every respect. His first lodging was at the Hotel Jacob, on the street of the same name, where Lewis Galantière welcomed them. In his enthusiasm, Ernest improvised a boxing match with him, breaking his glasses. He was creating his persona: active to the point of excess, he exerted a charm over people that stopped them from getting seriously angry with him. Later, he would break a window of the Hotel Gritti Palace in Venice and shoot a bullet from a revolver into a wall at the Ritz without incurring even a reprimand for either act. Deeds that would normally be unforgiveable were almost appreciated in Ernest: even his excesses seemed to lend people and places a little of his aura. At the beginning of January, the couple moved to 74 rue du Cardinal-Lemoine, where they would stay until 1924, when they settled into 113 rue Notre-Dame-des-Champs. Ernest began going to Shakespeare and Company on rue de l'Odéon, while Hadley took out a subscription to borrow its books; both were voracious readers. Ernest also started to frequent the Parisian cafés that would long serve as his writing places.

It was here, while sampling unfamiliar drinks and food, that he wrote his first successful stories. Café au lait, brioche, *pommes à l'huile, cervelas*, fried *goujons* of sole, Portuguese oysters, roast *poularde*, asparagus, and *tarte aux pommes* were some of the dishes that he consumed and transcribed into *A Moveable Feast*. He never omitted to mention the composition of meals, the names of wines or the brands of drinks. Thus, for example, during a trip to Switzerland, descriptions of the Rhône and the Dents du Midi mingle with those of *truite au bleu* and *vin d'Aigle* wrapped in a sheet of *La Gazette de Lausanne*. These details are not there just to add local color but sprang from a new method of composition: the names of streets or the brands of alcohol, such as Saint James rum, had more meaning for Ernest than great words charged with transcendental significance. The simple, flat vocabulary that gave his prose its disconcerting plainness was also inspired by Ernest's encounter with the modern art of Cézanne and Monet, whose work he would visit in the museums between walks in the streets or the Luxembourg gardens: "thinking inside himself that they had done with paint and canvas what he had been striving to do all morning." His encounter with this new culture enabled Ernest to develop a narrative technique that would become his hallmark. We gradually see adjectives and adverbs disappearing, sentences becoming incisive and rhythmic. Ernest rejected elegant variation in favor of quasi-obsessional repetition, Latin-based words being banished in favor of a monosyllabic Anglo-Saxon vocabulary that gave his work its distinctive staccato style. If light, rather than form, was the main feature of Monet's painting, Ernest's would be the names of places, of brands, of details that played the role of so many *objets trouvés* in his artistic creation. Like Cézanne, he sought to "break the fruit bowl" and abolish perspective to render things flat; just as the cubists would soon do by concentrating on primary shapes, he sought to strip language back to its base form, its constituent elements.

1. Portrait of the artist as a young man, in the 1920s.

Hadley was often left to her own devices in their poorly heated flat. Ernest was writing about Michigan: "After writing a story I was always empty and both sad and happy, as though I had made love." For him, writing was an act of taking possession that he associated with physical love from the male perspective — to the extent that his third wife, Martha, would remark that he was more interested in his books than in the women of his life. Writing took him to another realm, and its completion always represented a small death.

Ernest had come to Paris to write. True, he had brought with him from Chicago the fragments of a war novel and several ideas for stories, but Paris changed everything. He read Russian writers (Turgenev, Tolstoy and Dostoevsky), French writers (Stendhal, Flaubert and Maupassant) and the Anglo-American modernists, James Joyce, T.S. Eliot and Gertrude Stein. "But in Paris writing was a new game with Left Bank rules." Analogies between the couple's lives and Ernest's writing abound: they form the very warp and weft of their Parisian existence. And so when he wrote "hunger was good discipline," Ernest was referring as much to their stomachs as to the hunger that must push the young artist in his work, and *A Moveable Feast* (in its first version of 1964[2]) ended with the nostalgia-filled words: "[T]his is how Paris was in the early days when we were very poor and very happy." However, this portrait of the overburdened, malnourished artist was also a product of novelistic imagination. If the Hemingways could not lead the high life in Paris, they nonetheless did not live so badly, particularly due to the good exchange rate, then 12 francs to the dollar. One of Ernest's first dispatches to the *Star* was, moreover, on this subject: a bottle of wine cost 60 centimes, a breakfast 2.5 francs and everything else was just as cheap, enthused the young special envoy. Ernest, unlike numerous Americans in Paris — e.e. cummings, John Dos Passos, William Faulkner and so many others — was not immediately seduced by the Left Bank nonchalance. For all that Jake in *The Sun Also Rises* might declare that "[i]t is such an important part of the ethics [of a journalist] that you should never seem to be working," Ernest cultivated his professional side. In his article for the *Star* entitled "American Bohemians in Paris," he has nothing but harsh criticism for these "loafers," this "scum of Greenwich Village, New York, ... skimmed off and deposited in large ladles on that section of Paris adjacent to the Café Rotonde."

Ernest was preoccupied by his author's income. Hadley had an allowance of approximately 3,000 dollars a year; his income, representing only half that sum, was added to this. Ernest could certainly have survived and devoted a whole year to his writing without having to produce a word for the *Star*. But, while he associated writing with masculine power, he had grown up in a house dominated economically and psychologically by his mother, Grace. Without ever saying it explicitly, he would several times imply that she had pushed his father to suicide; when he went to demand his share of the inheritance, she replied that she had spent it on his education and travel. When Ernest reacted with surprise, "she didn't answer, but instead took me to see the lavish new music wing she had built on the house." And so the artistic hunger and discipline that Ernest forced on himself had origins that went far beyond the couple's financial situation and lay in Ernest's fear that material well-being would be fatal for him, or at least his talent.

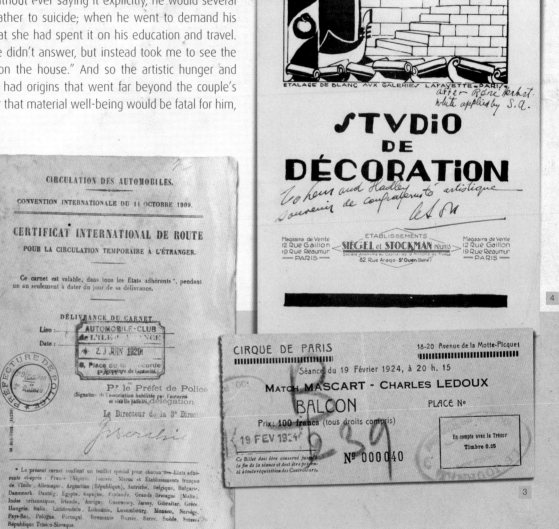

Souvenirs of Ernest's Parisian life: the tourist guide *Paris Seen in Four Days* (1), a car permit (2), a ticket for the boxing match between Mascart and Ledoux (3) and the brochure of an interior decorator signed "to Hem and Hadley" (4).

NOTE Foreword To Scott. (In Italics)

His talent was as natural as the pattern that was made

by the dust on a butterfly's wings. At ~~one~~ time he understood it

no more than the butterfly did and he did not know when it was brushed

or marred. He ~~even needed someone as a conscience and~~ <u>sometimes</u> he needed

~~professionals or normally educated people to make his writing legible~~

~~and not illiterate.~~ Later he became conscious of his damaged wings

and of their construction and he learned to think ~~and~~ But for a while he ~~could not fly~~

~~any more because the love of flight was gone and he could only think~~

of when it had been effortless. ~~In the meantime, thinking well and fully conscious of its worth, he had written The great gatsby & Tender Is The Night is a better book (written in heroic and desperate confession, at was the failure of there~~

He was flying again and ~~then~~ I was lucky to meet him just after a good time in his writing if not a good one in his life.

1. Staff of the Hotel Taube, where Ernest and Hadley stayed when they visited Schruns, Austria, 1925.

2. Hadley in Schruns, 1925.

3. A bearded Ernest; the sun and the cold irritated his sensitive skin, and he started to grow a beard that would become a distinguishing characteristic.

Paris became the Hemingways' home base, but the couple also ventured outside it. Their first trip to Chamby-sur-Montreux in Switzerland, undertaken the day after they moved to rue du Cardinal-Lemoine, enabled Ernest to discover landscapes that would play a central role in his life and that formed the backdrop to several stories and to *A Farewell to Arms*. They soon returned to the region with friends of Ernest's and, in the romantic footsteps of 18th-century travelers, walked across a still partially snow-covered St. Bernard's Pass toward Italy. Ernest also made several trips to Germany and to Austria, notably around Triberg, where he went trout fishing. He and Hadley visited the Black Forest, where they went on long hikes, but Ernest was disappointed by landscapes that he found insufficiently wild and picturesque; the high point of the trip would be their first air flight, between Bourget and Strasbourg, in a rattling old crate. Later, Ernest would rediscover Italy with great delight. At Cortina d'Ampezzo he again saw the Dolomites, first glimpsed in 1918; in Rapallo, they went to call on Ezra Pound, whom Ernest had met during his first months in Paris. In 1923 he began taking his first trips to Spain, on the instigation of Gertrude Stein, whom the Hemingways saw with great regularity. Spain — the next great source of inspiration in Ernest's life.

The Greco-Turkish War was coming to an end, against a backdrop of massacres and wholesale displacement of populations. Ernest went to Constantinople for three weeks, from where he returned so covered with lice that he had to shave his head; he also returned laden with presents to win over Hadley, who had been furious at his departure. The trip to Constantinople had earned him 400 dollars; in addition, Ezra Pound wanted him to get involved in an editorial project with the mock-funereal title of "Inquest into the state of contemporary English prose." Ernest was in high spirits. He felt that he was going to embark on serious writing. He had a book planned, in fragments, and had already written several stories. But all that had to wait because first he had to go back to Lausanne in Switzerland to cover the peace conference that would bring an end to hostilities and determine the borders of the new Greek and Turkish states. Having put all his current work into files, Ernest arrived in Switzerland on November 21, 1922. In Lausanne, he reported on the negotiations and laughed at the histrionic attitudes struck by Benito Mussolini, whom he described as holding a book to give himself a serious air; when he got closer, Ernest saw that "it was a French-English dictionary held upside down."

When the conference came to a close, Ernest asked Hadley — whom he had asked to join him any time she felt in a "traveling mood" — to come and spend several days in Switzerland to ski on the slopes above Lake Leman. Intending to please her husband, Hadley put all his manuscripts into a suitcase, including the carbon copies, and went to the Gare de Lyon. The exact details of what subsequently happened are shrouded in the fog that veils all traumatic events, but when she got off the train at Lausanne, Hadley was so overcome with tears that she could not speak to tell Ernest that his suitcase had been stolen and his manuscripts lost. Incredulous, he immediately jumped on the next train to Paris, where he alerted his friends and acquaintances and turned the apartment upside down — but all to no avail: the entire body of his first writing had been lost forever. He always refused to talk about how he spent that catastrophic night; the following day, he went to see Gertrude Stein and Alice B. Toklas, who consoled him over a wonderful lunch. In vain Ezra Pound tried to reassure him that the loss was a good thing; Ernest could not prevent the wound from smarting or refrain from taking what was, after all, just a blow of fate, as a betrayal.

He had long asked his friends to participate with him in winter sports. And so, on the slopes of La Dent de Lys and the Col de Jaman, he skied and bobsledded from morning to night in an attempt to forget. The beautiful story "Cross-Country Snow" would evoke this period and the peace of mind that Ernest had to learn to rediscover in himself. The theme of this story about skiing is the balance between freedom and responsibility, and in January 1923 Ernest felt more in need of such equilibrium than ever: Hadley was pregnant.

1. Bobsled run in Sonloup, in the upper slopes of Montreux, Switzerland. Everyone is focused on the turn, apart from Ernest at the back, who is smiling at the camera.

2. Ernest, Hadley and Bumby. Schruns, spring 1926.

3. Baptism certificate for John Hadley Nicanor Hemingway. His third name came from the famous torero Nicanor Villalta and is testament to Ernest's passion for bullfighting. John, known as "Bumby" or "Jack," would become the father of Margaux and Mariel Hemingway.

4. Bumby on his father's skis, 1924.

5. The track at Sonloup, with the Dents du Midi as a backdrop. This is the scenery of "Cross-Country Snow" and the last part of *A Farewell to Arms*.

From 1922, Gertrude "instructed" Ernest and her lessons dealt, as he would later describe, with writing and sex. Stein lived with a woman and in the 1920s and '30s she became a visible figure of lesbianism, not only in her own circle but also among the population at large. In Paris, Ernest encountered a world that was radically different from the puritan America he had left behind. The relaxed sexual mores, the general attitudes on what constituted good and evil, the racial mixing due both to the influx of people from the colonies and the numerous Afro-Americans fleeing the discriminatory Jim Crow laws, not to mention the alcohol that flowed liberally when, since 1922, America had been under the dry regime of Prohibition — all this was enough to disorient the young Ernest, who had realized "that everything I did not understand probably had something to it." The other great lesson he learned from Gertrude concerned writing and was expressed in a phrase that he would make his own and reflect on throughout his life: "Write the truest sentence you know." Truth and the real would from now on be connected to the stylistic austerity that Ernest would fine-tune in Spain using bullfighting as a metaphor. They would be a source of inspiration but also of doubt when, like the dying Harry in "The Snows of Kilimanjaro" or Thomas Hudson in *Islands in the Stream*, he feared he had wasted his talent and betrayed truth and the real.

In June and July 1923, Ernest went to Spain for the first time, and in August his first book was published: *Three Stories and Ten Poems*, which, as the title indicates, gathered three stories that had miraculously survived the loss of the manuscripts, including the sexually explicit "Up in Michigan," which Gertrude Stein found "inaccrochable" (i.e., "unhangable," in the sense of a painting that could not be displayed). In October, Hadley gave birth to John Hadley Nicanor Hemingway, whose godmothers were Gertrude and Alice and who was known as "Bumby" or "Jack." Although Ernest was close to Gertrude, their two strong egos would gradually turn the relationship into a difficult one. Ernest acknowledged that he had learned a lot from her but commented scornfully that she did not work on her prose enough. As for Gertrude, she would always feel that Ernest totally lacked modesty and self-control, always concerned with "the career, the career." When Gertrude reported a conversation in which she had heard the expression "the lost generation" and assumed it as her own, Hemingway denounced what he called "egotism and mental laziness versus discipline." Making reference to Stein's famous phrase "a rose is a rose is a rose," Hemingway mocked the mantra of the lost generation with his "Well, Gertrude ... a pronouncement, was a pronouncement, was a pronouncement." Ernest could not easily hurt those he liked; however, he did not pass up the opportunity to settle scores with Stein or Sherwood Anderson. He dealt the coup de grâce to the latter when, in 1926, he published a satirical novel, *The Torrents of Spring*, deriding his style.

Ernest had found the rhythm of both his life and his prose. This very distinctive style emerged in December 1923 with the proofs of *In Our Time*, the first major collection of his stories, which would be published in 1925 in New York. These stories still fascinate Hemingway's readers; they include the first appearances of Nick Adams, that incarnation of Ernest who would appear all through his work. The stories were separated by short, incisive essays, simple snatches of observations that were the first examples of Ernest's minimalist style. He also contributed to the *Little Review*, which would publish James Joyce's *Ulysses* in serial form, as well as works by numerous modernist artists. His growing prestige got him invited onto the editorial board of the *Transatlantic Review* directed by Ford Madox Ford.

1, 2, 4. Gertrude Stein and Alice B. Toklas, Bumby's godmothers, making a fuss of baby in the Luxembourg gardens, 1924. Hadley can also be seen.

3. Portrait of John ("Bumby"). Schruns, 1926.

Between trips to Schruns in Austria to ski and Spain, where he attended the San Fermín festival, Ernest developed a friendship and a rivalry with Scott Fitzgerald and his wife, Zelda. The very masculine concept that he then had of writing meant that he dismissed Zelda as mad while also admiring (not without a touch of jealousy) Scott's first major novel, *The Great Gatsby*. In 1925, it was his turn to write his first major novel, begun as a short story, *The Sun Also Rises*.

Interesting himself more and more in art, under the tutelage of Gertrude Stein, he acquired Joan Miró's *The Farm* (paying for it in installments), which he gave to Hadley. As in the previous year, Ernest and Hadley went skiing in the Austrian Voralberg. But unlike that year, Pauline Pfeiffer, whom he had met in the spring, was also there.

In March 1926, after going to New York, where he broke his contract with his first publisher and signed up with Scribner's, whom he would never leave, Ernest returned to Paris, where Pauline was. And while he was supposed to take the first train to Austria to rejoin Hadley, he wrote, "The girl I was in love with was in Paris then, and I did not take the first train, or the second or the third." The marriage with Hadley ended in March 1927, prompting Ernest to conclude in *A Moveable Feast*: "All things truly wicked start from an innocence."

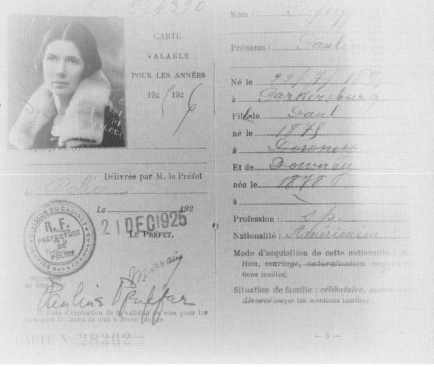

Opposite page: Gstaad, Switzerland, February 1927. Ernest sends the photo to his publisher, writing on the back: "This is to reassure you if you hear reports of another of your authors dying of drink."

1, 2. Pauline, Gstaad, 1927.

3. Pauline Pfeiffer's French identity papers.

THE CAPITAL
OF THE WORLD

Writing and Death

Before his first trip to Spain, in June and July of 1923, Ernest had already encountered, or at least glimpsed, the peninsula on two occasions. The first was during his return from the Austro-Italian front in 1919, when the *Giuseppe Verdi* put into port at Algeciras and the second, just two years earlier, during the crossing to France with Hadley, when they stopped over at Vigo, which he described in a letter to his friend Bill Smith as "the dream place for a man." Brief as they were, these visits left Ernest, who had an unshakeable belief in his luck and his instinct, with the lasting impression of an exotic country imbued with a powerful imaginative force. And indeed, Spain would be for him a land of discovery.

His first Spanish period occurred during his Parisian years, when he was mingling with the pack of apprentice writers, with their more or less well-intentioned patrons and luminaries such as Gertrude Stein and Ezra Pound. As he would say in *Death in the Afternoon*: "I was trying to learn to write, commencing with the simplest things, and one of the simplest things and the most fundamental is violent death." This book, which he wrote in Key West, Florida, after his first series of visits to Spain, is offered as a *vade mecum* aimed at Americans who want to know more about bullfighting. From the very beginning, Ernest acknowledges that he has no doubt that from a modern, moral point of view, or a Christian one, "the whole bullfight is indefensible." The man whom the Spanish would baptize "Don Ernesto" thus did not seek to defend bullfighting but to write "a serious book on such an unmoral subject." But if Ernest was writing about bullfighting in *Death in the Afternoon*, the book is also, above all, his theory of literary creation, his central work about the art of writing. This apprenticeship of "the simplest and the most fundamental" aspects of the writing he would do in Spain would in a sense constitute his literary school–leaving certificate.

It was on the advice of Gertrude Stein that Ernest and his friends Bill Bird and Bob McAlmon left for Madrid; the wealthy McAlmon paid for the trip, which did not stop Ernest from behaving obnoxiously to him and reproaching him for what he called his romantic sensibility when he looked away, horrified by the spectacle of horses (which, in that period, did not wear the protective caparison) being disemboweled in the arena. For Ernest was adamant: one had to look death straight in the face, without turning away. In a strikingly cruel image, he added that a writer should make death visible and not "physically or mentally shut his eyes, as one might do if he saw a child that he could not possibly reach or aid, about to be struck by a train." This infanticidal image recalls the cruelty of war and of stories such as "On the Quai at Smyrna"; like war, the bullfight is the occasion for a brutal discovery of the world.

Opposite page: The matador Chicuelo. Photo chosen by Ernest for *Death in the Afternoon*. According to Ernest, Chicuelo's aestheticism made him one of the masters of the modern *faena*. This did not stop him criticizing Chicuelo severely because he "hated killing" — and the killing of the bull was that "moment of truth" that Ernest sought to capture.

1. Arrival of the bulls in the Pamplona arena at the end of the *encierro*.

2. The aficionados testing their courage and talent. On the right, the man challenging the bull with a jacket is Ernest, during the San Fermín festival of 1925.

3. Some of the toreros admired by Ernest: from left to right, Rafael Gómez y Ortega, known as "El Gallo," his brother José, known as "Joselito"; we can also see the banderillero Enrique Berenguet, known as "Blanquet," and, far right, the torero Paco Madrid of Malaga.

Ernest is not interested in the picturesque, touristic delights of Spain: "more flamingos! [sic]," he exclaimed several times as the three friends explored Andalucía. Meanwhile, they attended their first novillada[3] in Madrid and their first great bullfight in Seville. Responding to what was perhaps already his sense of the tragic in life, Ernest was very soon persuaded that bullfighting was not a sport but a tragedy. As the Andalucían poet Federico García Lorca wrote during the same period: "Spain is the only country in which death is a national spectacle."[4] Ernest, who came from a country whose national pastime was baseball, understood the importance of what he was experiencing. And thus his judgment of his own culture was severe, seen through the prism of the *duende* described by Lorca. We Americans, he wrote, "are not fascinated by death, its nearness and avoidance. We are fascinated by victory and we replace the avoidance of death by the avoidance of defeat." Taking death seriously — something American culture was incapable of — was the challenge posed by this discovery, which had to be written about.

And thus visits to Spain took place every year from 1923 to 1933, apart from 1928 and 1932, the year *Death in the Afternoon* was published. The short essays inserted into *In Our Time* also date from this first Spanish period, as well as disquieting and moving stories like "The Capital of the World," "A Clean, Well-Lighted Place" and, particularly, Ernest's first great novel, *The Sun Also Rises*. The second period was that of the Spanish Civil War, which Ernest and his third wife, Martha, described as reporters and which he would evoke in *For Whom the Bell Tolls* and "The Fifth Column" in particular. And then, finally, there was the last seven years of his life during which Ernest would return to Spain to attend numerous bullfights and to write *The Dangerous Summer*, a chronicle of the fatal *mano a mano* between the bullfighters Luis Miguel Dominguín and Antonio Ordóñez.

N o sooner had he come back from his first trip to Spain than Ernest was yearning to return. He managed to infect Hadley with his enthusiasm, and she duly declared that watching bullfighting might be beneficial to the baby she was carrying. And so in 1924, Ernest, his wife and some friends descended on the Hotel Quintana in Pamplona, which would become their headquarters. Ernest discovered the *feria* of San Fermín with its Catholic processions, an extraordinary spectacle for the well-brought-up Protestant that he was, its *riau-riau*, noisy pagan dances, alcoholic excesses and drunken revels, and then the bullfights that took place every morning before the *encierro*, that frenzied run over 1 mile (2 km) in which death-defying young men would approach, and narrowly escape, the dagger-sharp horns of the bulls launched in their pursuit. Ernest also took part in this mad run and was slightly wounded, inciting the *Chicago Tribune* to recount his exploits with the headline "Bull Gores 2 Yanks Acting As Toreadors." Ernest popularized San Fermín, and tourists have since flocked there every year in their thousands in an attempt to recapture its atmosphere — if only, in Michel Leiris's words, to encounter "the shadow of a bull's horn."

Ernest was not alone in Spain during the 1920s and '30s. Other than the friends he brought along with him, the entire modernist movement was crowding into the *barreras*, the front rows of the arena. From 1910, Pablo Picasso, a native Andalucían and great aficionado of the bullfight, initiated Georges Braque and Max Jacob to tauromachy. Gertrude Stein, a close friend of Picasso's and one of the first admirers of his art, got involved in the bullfighting world through the artist. Later, it would be the poets Jean Cocteau, Paul Eluard and René Char; the painters Francis Picabia, André Masson and Francis Bacon; the novelists Hemingway and Dos Passos, of course, but also Henri de Monterlant and Georges Bataille, as well as thinkers like Michel Leiris: a whole intellectual world in search of ethical and aesthetic values that had been lost in the mud of wars and the haze of depressions that flowed into the bullfighting ring.

Ernest and Hadley, still anonymous spectatators, in the first row. Pamplona, 1925.

I n 1924, in the company of Bill Bird and Bob McAlmon, Ernest went on a walking tour in the Pyrenees from Burguete to Andorra, covering some 185 miles (300 km) in four days. As usual, he slightly exaggerated his physical performance during the walk, which would become the material for *The Sun Also Rises*, in which three companions undertake a similar trip. The journey to Spain, on these paths near the Compostella route, has nothing to do with tourism but it is indeed, as the novel suggests, a pilgrimage and a rite of passage. The following year, in Pamplona, the central figure of this novel entered Ernest's life when Lady Duff Twysden joined the Hemingways. In the middle of a divorce from the English baronet from whom she had her title, Lady Twysden was spectacularly beautiful, sporting a boyish haircut and a razor-sharp intelligence; she would become Brett Ashley, and Jake would say on seeing her for the first time: "She was built with curves like the hull of a racing yacht, and you missed none of it with that wool jersey." It is not certain that she and Ernest had an affair, but she did have one with his friend Harold Loeb. Ernest was seething with rage and jealousy, and in the novel, Loeb, who came from a wealthy New York Jewish family, became Cohn, mocked by the anti-Semitic narrator Jake Barnes.

In Madrid, Ernest again attended bullfights, refining his aficionado's eye and weaving an ever-closer connection between the matador's art and that of the writer. "Nobody ever lives their lives all the way up except bullfighters," declared Jake in *The Sun Also Rises*, and the character of the matador Pedro Romero is testament to that in the novel, which Ernest was writing furiously that summer of 1925; on September 15, a first manuscript was completed. But, Ernest realized, bullfighting did not just involve killing bulls to the musical accompaniment of a pasodoble while wearing pink tights. Writing of Madrid, he observed that it was only here that the essence of Spain could be found for "there is not one local-colored place for tourists in town." The Prado alone justified the journey but, he added, "when you can have the Prado and the bullfight season at the same time, with the Escurial not two hours to the north and Toledo to the south ... it makes you feel badly, all question of immortality aside, to know that you will have to die and never see it again." Here he is developing the notion of the bullfight as metaphor for art and as expression of the human condition. In the brutality of the bullfight, Ernest saw a wounded humanity in the grip of its mortality, and it is this that he wanted, like the bullfighter, to put down in writing; Ernest could have quoted Georges Bataille: "because we are human and we live in the dark shadow of death, we experience the frustrated, desperate violence of eroticism."

1. Hiking near Pamplona, 1925.

2. The spectacular city of Ronda in Andalucía, cradle of the torero dynasty of the Romeros, who would often welcome Ernest to their home.

3. Several characters in search of an author; Ernest would also use them in *The Sun Also Rises*. From left to right: Jake Barnes (Ernest, in the foreground), Brett Ashley (Lady Duff Twysden, beside Ernest) Robert Cohn (Harold Loeb, at the back). We can also see Hadley (full face), Don Stewart and Pat Guthrie (friends of the Hemingways). Pamplona, 1925.

4. In the bullring of Ronda.

5. Picnic near Pamplona, 1925.

6. Ronda, before the corrida.

7. Ernest and a creature with impressive horns — but it is an ox and not a bull. San Sebastian, summer 1927.

rnest began to acquire a deep knowledge of the world of bulls, and his Spanish greatly improved. He read many magazines and frequented the *mundillo* of aficionados, matadors and owners. If experts remained divided on the question of his expertise in the domain, most agreed that he had a sure, critical eye. But Ernest was above all a writer, and his observations always referred less to tauromachy than to the art of fiction. Just as he sought the simplest possible sentence to get as close as possible to the truth in his writing, he wanted to write like the matador who "is performing a work of art and ... is playing with death, bringing it closer, closer, closer to himself, a death that you know is in the horns." Relinquishing the foreplay of cape and *muleta*, as he makes clear in *Death in the Afternoon*, Ernest was above all interested in the killing of the bull, "the final sword thrust, the actual encounter between the man and the animal, what the Spanish call the moment of truth." This moment lasted only a fraction of a second; practically invisible and evanescent, it was, however, the crux, for the matador, Goya or Hemingway, that made art permanent. At the moment of truth, reality appears "that flash when man and bull form one figure as the sword goes all the way in." The moment of truth is the moment of death, and it is also the climax to which the whole preceding dance of seduction has led. This theme had appeared in Picasso's work, culminating in his *Guernica*, in which intertwined bodies are carried off by orgasm and death; for Ernest, too, death as the keystone of writing would become an obsessive theme.

Opposite page: The arena filled with cushions after a fine *bronca*: the torero has not done his job.

1. Ernest and Pauline in the ring. Ernest seems to be the only one following the *lidia* — but perhaps he has spotted the photographer. Pamplona, 1928.

2. The *tercio* (third) lancing: until 1928 the horses did not wear a protective cover. "I told her about watching the bull, not the horse, when the bulls charged the picadors, and got her to watching the picador place the point of his pic," Jake says about Brett in *The Sun Also Rises*.

3. The work of the *muleta*; the torero gets the bull's horns close to him. Note the dead horses in the background.

4. The *tercio* (third) killing: the corrida "is an art that deals with death and death wipes it out," wrote Ernest.

PAMPLONA
1924

FERIAS Y FIESTAS DE SAN FERMIN

Programa de festejos que se celebrarán
del 6 al 18 de Julio

PLAZA · DE · TOROS
PAMPLONA
1923
Contrabarrera N.º 21
Puerta 10
SOMBRA
Ptas. 7,20
Prueba · 9 de Julio

PLAZA · DE · TOROS
PAMPLONA
1923
Contrabarrera N.º 22
Puerta 10
SOMBRA
Ptas. 7,20
incluidos impuestos
TENDIDO 1
Consérvese esta
parte del billete
Prueba · 9 de Julio

Souvenirs of Hemingway the aficionado:
program and tickets for the corrida (1, 2),
train ticket for Pamplona (3) and Spanish
fishing permit (4).

Hadley, for her part, relaxed at Juan-les-Pins in the south of France, in the company of the Fitzgeralds in the home of wealthy friends who considered the Hemingways part of the family. There she met Pauline and Virginie Pfeiffer. Pauline wrote for *Vogue* and became a good friend of Hadley's; she had, on the other hand, nothing but harsh words for Ernest, whom she considered arrogant and full of himself. Daughters of a good family, well heeled and basically free from the constraints of work, the Pfeiffer sisters did not hesitate to join the Hemingways first on the Côte d'Azur, then for winter sports in Schruns in Austria and finally in Pamplona for the San Fermín festival of 1926. Pauline and Ernest lost little time in embarking on an amorous adventure, which, like a bullfight, was "stimulating and fun" at the beginning, as he wrote in *A Moveable Feast*, and "goes on that way for a while." But bullfighting had also taught Ernest that "all stories, if continued far enough, end up in death, and he is no true story-teller who would keep that from you." This story was over; the death of his first marriage merged with the eroticism and promise of the new encounter, which had to involve the necessarily cruel sacrifice of a victim.

This dangerous summer was followed by that of 1927 in which, after a honeymoon in France, at Grau-du-Roi in Camargue, the now-married Ernest and Pauline returned to Spain. Ernest came back bursting with plans, and notes, for his new book, which he described to Max Perkins, the editor at Scribner's, "as a sort of Arabia Deserta ... on tauromachy." Pauline, who had just turned 32, came back from Spain pregnant.

And so, in 1928 there was no trip to Pamplona, Pauline wanting to give birth in the United States. After stopping over in Cuba, the couple weighed anchor in Key West, which was then a small, tranquil island at the southernmost extreme of the country. Pauline gave birth to Patrick in Kansas City on June 28; in July, Ernest left to go fishing in Wyoming. He missed Spain. He spent the winter working on what would become *A Farewell to Arms*, but as soon as April came, the couple got on a ship in Cuba bound first for France and then Pamplona. Ernest enthusiastically followed the bullfights of the *temporada*. After exploring the length and breadth of the peninsula with his wife in their gleaming Ford roadster, sign of his new celebrity, he went to Madrid in September to watch, then meet, a matador from, of all places, Brooklyn. His name was Sidney Franklin and he and Ernest became friends. A eulogistic portrait is painted of him in *Death in the Afternoon* — a portrait that many bullfighting specialists found inaccurately flattering.

1. Ernest and the Brooklyn torero Sidney Franklin on board the *Paris*, 1937.

2. Ernest and Sidney Franklin in front of the Castle of Manzanares el Real, 1929, the year of their meeting.

The following years were marked by the climate of insurrection that reigned in Spain on the eve of the civil war. The bullfight became a political pawn that both pro- and anti-Franco supporters attempted to use to their advantage. This did not prevent Ernest from writing to his friend the painter Waldo Peirce that the revolution in Spain was awfully nice and that he hated ditching the *percebes* to go back to America. In 1932, *Death in the Afternoon* appeared; Ernest made a short trip to Madrid in 1933, but his gaze was already fixed on new pastures.

And, in 1933, Ernest fell in love with Africa. Spain's gold seemed to have been mined, and it now moved, along with bullfighting, into the background. He finished the moving short story "The Capital of the World" in Key West, while Spain entered the torment of civil war. When he went back in 1937 and 1938, it was as a war reporter with the woman who became his third wife, Martha. His last visits, in the 1950s, would be in the company of Mary, his last wife.

Fifteen years after his most recent visit there, at the end of the 1950s it was a very different Ernest who returned to a Spain that had also changed. Under the yoke of Franco, the country was an ally of the United States, and it was now easy to visit; it was not always easy to travel in Spain because of its poor infrastructures, but it was very inexpensive, thanks to the exchange rate, and was still undeveloped. On the other hand, the country did not welcome former opponents of Franco with open arms. In *The Dangerous Summer*, Ernest fantasized about a spectacular political denouement as he went over the border from France to Spain; on this journey, he happened on a customs officer who was one of his readers and admirers, and he crossed the border without a hitch. In Pamplona, which he wanted to show to Mary, Ernest scrupulously attended all the ceremonies of the festival and saw Antonio Ordóñez, son of Niño de la Palma — the model for Pedro Romero in *The Sun Also Rises* — fight for the first time; Ordóñez, with Luis Dominguín, whom he lost no time in meeting, would be at the center of *The Dangerous Summer*.

In 1952 Ernest received the Pulitzer Prize for *The Old Man and the Sea*, and films featuring every Hollywood star — Humphrey Bogart and Lauren Bacall, Burt Lancaster and Ava Gardner, Gregory Peck and Joan Bennett, Gary Cooper and Ingrid Bergman — had managed to establish his reputation as the most famous writer of the 20th century in a way his books had not (yet) achieved. In Spain he was also recognized everywhere. Matadors dedicated bulls to him. Wherever he went, people jostled to see him, and his presence in the arena formed part of the spectacle; reporters published his photo in articles on the bullfight. In 1954, his status as literary hero was definitively confirmed when he received the Nobel Prize in Literature.

1. Autograph session after the corrida. Valencia arena, 1959.

2. The fiesta in full swing, Feria of Pamplona, 1959.

3. Like the toreros, Ernest was also a star outside the ring: here with an awed admirer, Valencia, 1959.

1. The protagonists of *The Dangerous Summer*. Brothers-in-law in private life, brothers in arms and duelists in the bullring: Antonio Ordóñez (foreground) and Luis Miguel Dominguín.

2. Dominguín greets the crowd at the end of a fight, his costume stained with the bull's blood.

3. Ernest (and Mary) in the ring, 1959. Ordóñez "dedicates" a bull to him by throwing him his *montera* (his hat), which Ernest is getting ready to catch.

4. Ordóñez confronting the bull; Ernest said of him that he loved to speak of the *faena* as "writing."

Right: Ordóñez comes over to talk to "Don Ernesto," and everyone cranes their necks to catch a glimpse of the two *fenómenos*. August 1959.

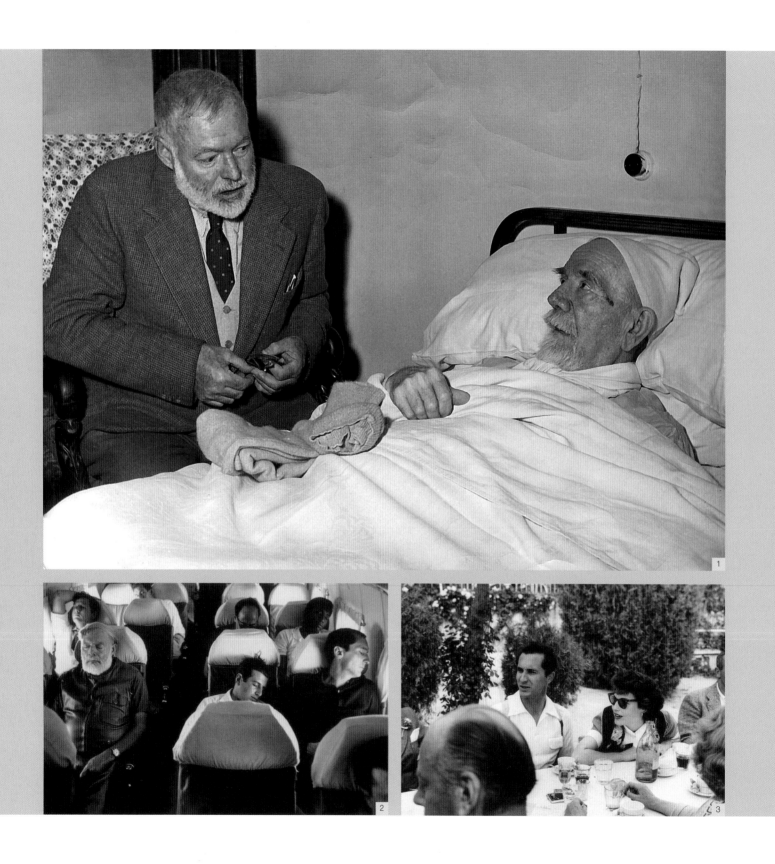

Africa continued to seduce Ernest, who doubtless wanted to show Mary his old haunts. Just before winning the Nobel Prize, he miraculously survived two successive airplane crashes there (although they had lasting effects that would eventually get the better of him). He again followed the *temporada*, this time with a traveling companion who would accompany him during the last years of his life and contribute to forging the Hemingway legend: Aaron Hotchner, who met Ernest in 1948, collected notes and anecdotes that he would reproduce in *Papa Hemingway*. It was during this journey that Ernest met Ava Gardner, just embarking on an affair with Luis Domínguin, who invited all of them to his property for a *tienta*, an event in which the mettle of young calves, future fighting bulls, is tested. Ernest also visited, like an ordinary Hemingway reader, the sites of *For Whom the Bell Tolls* — once again, fiction took over from reality in his life.

Increasingly victim to bouts of anxiety and panic about writer's block, Ernest did not go to Spain for nearly two years, but Spain came to him in the person of Ordóñez and Domínguin, who visited him at the Finca Vigía in 1955. When he went back to Spain at the end of the season in 1956, he attended bullfights involving the two brothers-in-law, but this trip would be most notable for his visit to Pío Baroja, a figure of the "Generation of 98" and a master admired by Ernest as well as a whole generation of writers, who was on his deathbed.

"One generation passeth away, and another generation cometh; but the earth abideth forever. The sun also ariseth, and the sun goeth down, and hasteth to the place where he arose," Ernest wrote, quoting Ecclesiastes, in an epigraph to *The Sun Also Rises*. The death of the old lion of the Spanish novel heralded the arrival of another generation, Ernest's. In 1959, he ran his last great lap of the circuit, a victory lap given to the matador who has fought with grace and dignity, with all his *pundonor*. As Hotchner wrote: "Old wine in its cask sometimes reacts to seasons, and the summer of 1959 was, by Ernest's own avowal, one of the best seasons of his life." This would be the memorable trip that would have him crossing and recrossing Spain to follow the *mano a mano* between Ordóñez and Domínguin, each of whom wanted to go down in the history books as the greatest matador that had ever lived. Sometimes traveling in the company of *cuadrillas*, matadors and their teams, Ernest chronicled this fight to the death in *The Dangerous Summer*, during which the two matadors several times experienced the bull's horns piercing their flesh.

There would be no real victor in this fratricidal struggle, Domínguin eventually being so badly wounded that he had to bow out of the competition. Ernest went to see him in hospital and stayed a long time at his bedside; Domínguin lived but on the way back Ernest commented sadly to his friend "Hotch": "Why the hell do the good and brave have to die before everyone else?"

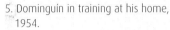

1. Ernest's visit with Pío Baroja, master of the Spanish novel, on his deathbed, October 1956. Soon afterward, a visibly moved Ernest attended his funeral.

2. Journey with Ordóñez and Domínguin in the fast *temporada* train. August 1959.

3. Domínguin and Ava Gardner, one of his numerous conquests. Costa del Sol, 1959.

4. A moment of relaxation with Ordóñez, minus his bullfighting costume, near the swimming pool of La Consula, 1959.

5. Domínguin in training at his home, 1954.

1. Ava Gardner and Ernest during a tienta on Domínguin's property, 1954.

2, 3. *Feria* of Pamplona, 1959.

Opposite page: End of the corrida.

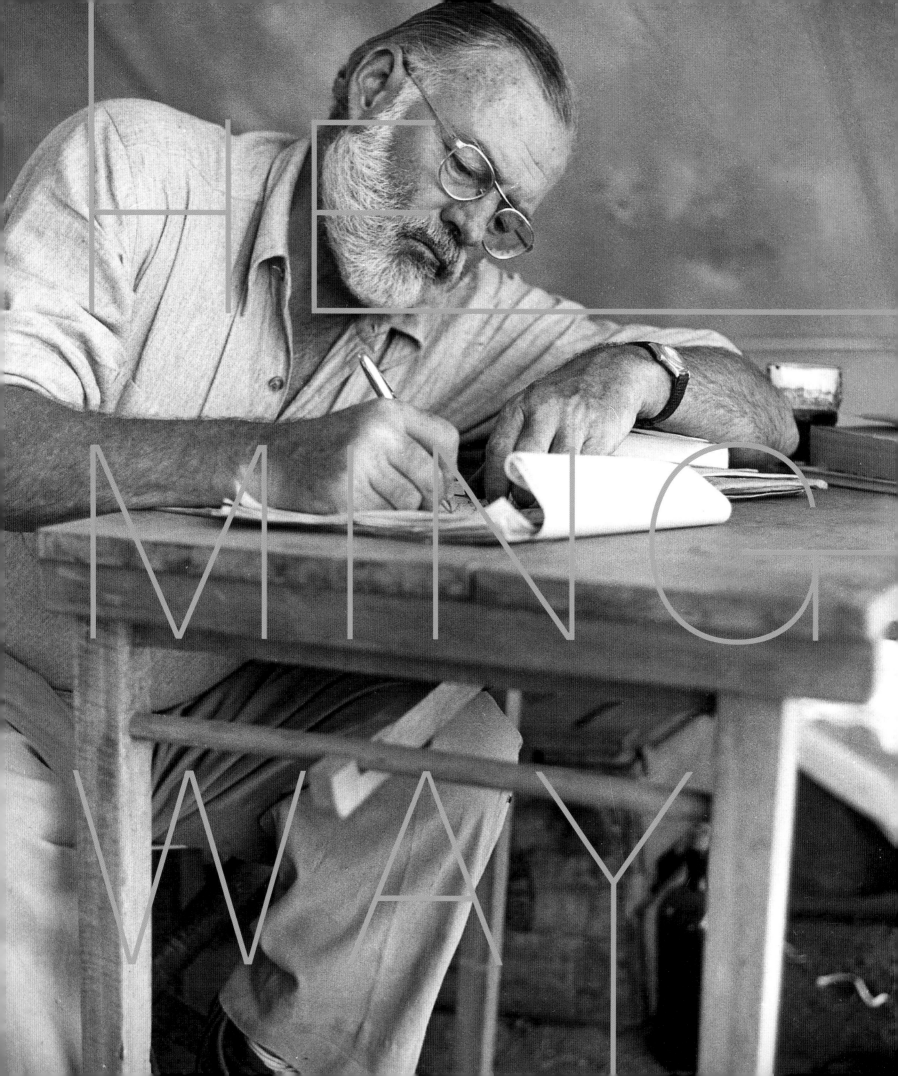

THE SNOWS OF KILIMANJARO

Africa, the Last Frontier

"Never wrote so directly of myself as in ['The Snows of Kilimanjaro']," declared Ernest in 1955 to his friend and confidant "Hotch" while they were staying at Key West in the small house where the writer had composed the story nearly 20 years earlier. He added that it was "as good as I've any right to be." Indeed, it was so good that for a long time afterward he would not be able to write, so much experience and emotion had he concentrated into it. Ernest published "Snows" in 1936, just a year after *Green Hills of Africa*, which retraced his first African experience. The book initially received a very lukewarm welcome. It begins with an anonymous quotation about the carcass of a leopard found frozen and dried out in the snows of the mountain the Massai called "the House of God." "No one has explained what the leopard was seeking at that altitude," concluded the quotation borrowed from the work[5] of a geologist who was the first European to reach the summit. But Ernest had changed the animal: the antelope of the original became a leopard in his story — the ruminant had become a solitary predator. The leopard had perhaps followed a track that had eventually got him lost. Similarly, what traces had led Ernest to Africa?

There would be two safaris, in Kenya and in Tanganyika. On the first, Ernest was 34; he had just married Pauline and was a rising literary star. His new wife's uncle had advanced the couple the exorbitant sum needed to pay for this luxury outing into the wilds. On the second safari, Ernest was 54 and accompanied by his fourth wife, Mary; he returned to the slopes of Africa's highest mountain, kitted out from head to toe in Abercrombie & Fitch, the outdoor-wear label worn by presidents and stars. In the years between the two trips, life, love, alcohol, combat, sickness, accidents, public pressure and the anxiety of writer's block had all taken their toll. If the first trip was a young man's exploration of new limits and entry into an unknown territory, the second was a return to places haunted by memory but also by fear of old age and death.

Opposite page: Ernest alone with the "House of God" behind him during the safari of 1953.

1. Young Ernest with his lion, 1934.

In any event, it was from these two safaris that much of the popular image of "Hemingway" would emerge — as well as the occasionally brutal reactions provoked by the khaki-wearing author. He had been seen in Bimini, Florida, fishing marlin and on the sand track around bullfighting arenas. If some were fascinated by him (particularly men who wanted to resemble him, even physically), others began to find this rather too colorful character disturbing, with all his posturing as a virile, triumphant Western male. In 1933, he came to blows with a good friend, the New York publisher Max Eastman, because the latter had published an article about *Death in the Afternoon* entitled "Bull in the Afternoon" — "bull" alluding to vainglorious nonsense, of course. As certain critics would later do, Eastman suggested that Ernest was so uncertain of his masculinity and his virility that he was protesting too much. To this criticism was added that of numerous intellectuals who found it absurd that in a dire recession that had left thousands in ruin and thrown thousands of others out of their homes to go pick what Steinbeck would call "the grapes of wrath," and in a world heading straight for the throes of a Second World War, a writer of Ernest's stature was lazing around on yachts fishing in the Caribbean, enjoying the spectacle of a bull being tortured in Spain or slaughtering animals for pleasure in an Africa that was in the grip of famine.

1, 3. Brief journey through Suez, and Ernest's first glimpses of Africa, en route for his first safari, 1933.

2. Several trophies of oryx and kudu, with the characters of Green Hills of Africa: Ben Fourie, Charles Thompson, Philip Percival (the white hunter) and Ernest. Tanganyika, 1934.

4. Pauline and "her" lion, which Ernest had to shoot, 1934.

5, 6. Ernest and his rhinoceros, the same year.

The African trail that Ernest was following had begun in his childhood, with the accounts of Teddy Roosevelt's 1909 safari. And indeed, Philip Percival, the very man who had been the guide for the former president, would be the white hunter of the 1934 expedition! Like that of Roosevelt, the explorer and creator of myths about the American West, Ernest's first safari was an opportunity to display his masculine prowess in a terrain that seemed like the last frontier of the conquering white male. The Nobel Prize–winning novelist and South African activist Nadine Gordimer declared that Ernest loved Africa but that, overtaken by emotion, he had constructed an Africa in the image of his desires and needs that bore little relationship to reality. Similarly, Toni Morrison, the African-American writer who is herself a Nobel Prize winner, recognized that she had learned some important things from Hemingway's writing but criticized him for having emptied Africa of its inhabitants or peopled it with invisible beings.

The trip began in territory that had been home to Karen Blixen, whose *Out of Africa* Hemingway had read with admiration. In January 1934, the hunt was fruitful but Ernest was suffering from dysentery, "this most noisome of diseases, which made every victory a disappointment and converted every minor failure into a catastrophe." To let off steam, he shot at his hated hyenas, just like the dying Harry in "The Snows of Kilimanjaro," who, when he sees a hyena passing in the distance moans, "That bastard crosses there every night, ... Every night for two weeks." Both men shot at hyenas to avenge themselves on the sickness tormenting their body — Harry's gangrene in fiction and Ernest's dysentery in reality — and on the life that was deserting them. In the preface of *Green Hills of Africa*, Ernest wrote that the goal of this "absolutely true book" was to see whether the depiction of real events could, if it was done in absolutely authentic fashion, "compete with a work of the imagination." If the "unchartered territory" of Africa lay principally in writing, Ernest's tortured intestines and Harry's gangrene reminded them both of the limits of their fantasies of power.

The hunt was almost too easy. Ernest was disappointed by the sluggish passivity of the buffalo; his joy at bagging his lion was dimmed by the shame of seeing the big cat lying at his feet, tormented by flies. As for the lion that he had brought down after Pauline had missed him at point-blank range, celebrating a shot that his wife had bungled left him with the bitter impression of betrayal and falsehood. A female antelope killed in error and a badly shot male who then had to be given over to the howling hyenas completed his disillusionment. Reality was disappointing.

There was also the exhilaration of the hunt and its trophies. But here too there was a snag: the size of the trophy was all-important. In *Green Hills of Africa*, Ernest depicted those laughably adolescent scenes reminiscent of the passages in *A Moveable Feast* in which he recounted that Scott Fitzgerald, uncertain of the adequacy of his male equipment, did the rounds of the museums with Ernest to reassure himself that he was indeed of normal size. To settle this "matter of measurements," the two men even went as far as comparing their masculine attributes in the toilets, with Ernest reassuring Scott that "there's nothing wrong with you." In Africa, this competitiveness reemerged. Ernest was upset when he realized that the biggest of the two horns of his black rhinoceros was barely as big as the smallest killed by his friend Charles Thompson and then was "poisoned with envy" when he saw that the horns of his kudu, that large antelope with twisted horns, were barely half the size of those bagged by the man who had become his best enemy. It was in vain that Percival tried to reassure him that "inches don't mean anything at all"; Ernest lived in a world of fantasy in which size mattered, and he knew that it was impossible not to feel competitive in this game between dominant males even if, as Percival said in the last act of this theater of masculinity,[6] it "spoils everything."

Just as in mankind's distant past, the trophies and their size bore testimony to the virile power of the hunter. However, the book is above all a morality play, as demonstrated by the presentation of the characters in *Green Hills*. The Africa recounted by Ernest is a continent that "the foreigner destroys"; Ernest was already fantasizing about returning to Africa, but no longer as a predator: "I would come back to Africa, but not to make a living of it ... I would come back to where it pleased me to live; to really live. Not just let my life pass. Our people went to America because that was the place to go then," said Hemingway. Ernest's Africa constituted a "pursuit of happiness," with all the metaphysical meaning that the expression had for an American, but it was a pursuit that occurred through the "displacement" of writing; the continent had to become a theater and their adventure a moral drama.

Ernest's safari came to a temporary halt when he had to be taken urgently to Nairobi for treatment of the dysentery that threatened to kill him. Once back in the bush, he returned to the hunt but the gray, humid skies heralded the approaching rainy season. The journey was long and bumpy, from track to train, train to boat, more boats, more trains. "A continent ages quickly once we come"; countries wore out and fell to dust like their inhabitants, news of the day and details of consumed lives would not even be footnotes in the book of history, but Africa remained, "for we have been there in the books and out of the books — and where we go, if we are any good, there you can go as we have been."

Opposite page:
View of Kilimanjaro, 1953. The snow on the summit was still plentiful.

I f on his return to the American continent Ernest had insomnia and was, as he wrote in *Green Hills*, homesick for Africa, if he already missed it like a woman to whom he had just made love and who moved away from him in the depression and "little death" following orgasm, it was because the dreamed-of next trip could be nothing more than a physical separation and a detour via writing. And so it was at Key West that he wrote about Africa, following the now well-known formula in which he wrote about Michigan in Paris, about Paris in Cuba and about Spain in Florida — life was always somewhere else. The territory that Ernest dreamed of exploring — and perhaps of appropriating — was that of writing, which, like Africa, "you can have, and you want more and more, to have, and be, and live in, to possess now again and always, for that sudden-ended always."

In 1952, Daryl Zanuck's film adaptation of "The Snows of Kilimanjaro" was released, starring Gregory Peck and Ava Gardner in the principal roles. It included a "small change," however: instead of ending with Harry's death, he was taken off in a plane (like the sick Ernest) and disappeared into the clouds, half-man, half-angel. "Once they make a purchase," Ingrid Bergman commented about the producers, "they only care about box office ... and the last person they value is the writer." When reality caught up with Ernest, it was always a disappointment. From Cuba, where he lived permanently, he had overseen the publication of the poorly received *Across the River and Into the Trees* two years earlier and then launched into *Islands in the Stream*, but he was making slow progress with it. Ernest, filled with doubts since the critical failure of his last novel, feared that he had lost his touch. His mother died in Memphis in June 1951, and in the same year, in which he had a stormy conversation with Pauline about their son Patrick, Pauline died in Los Angeles, after an internal hemorrhage. In February 1952, it was the turn of his publisher Charles Scribner to die in New York.

Not until *The Old Man and the Sea* would Ernest be reconciled with the critics and his mind finally put at rest: five million copies of the *Life* magazine in which the novel first appeared were sold, with Scribner's then publishing another 50,000 copies of the book. In June 1953, Ernest left Havana, where Batista had taken power, and sailed for New York then Paris and Spain, where he went back to Pamplona, Segovia and Madrid. But it was to Africa that he finally returned, putting an end to three years of drifting from island to island without setting foot on the continent. Ernest hoped that Africa would now be his terra firma.

1. Ernest and Mary at bedtime, 1953.

2, 3, 4. Ernest writing in the camp; Earl Theisen's photos for *Look* would seal the Hemingway image.

5. Mary and Ernest taking in and feeding a baby gazelle.

1. Ernest leaves for the hunt; the light and the composition of the image are reminiscent of those of Ernest the writer. The pen and the gun were associated in the collective image of the figure of Hemingway.

2. Image within an image: we forget that photos are often the staging of a scene.

3. Lying in wait for a rhinoceros.

Opposite page: Ernest and his buffalo, 1953.

In Mombassa, Kenya, he met up with his son Patrick, who owned a large estate near Dar es Salaam in Tanzania. After graduating with first-class honors in history and literature from Harvard, Patrick had become a white hunter. He would edit the book, which Ernest called his "African journal," that had emerged from the safari but which his father could not finish; it would not be published until 1999, under the title *True at First Light*. Philip Percival was also there; he had remained in contact with Ernest and now guided him for the second time. After Roosevelt, the white hunter would accompany the man who had in turn become an American figurehead. Having received the Pulitzer Prize for *The Old Man and the Sea*, Ernest signed a handsome contract for the film adaptation as well as a series of articles by *Look*, with its star photographer Earl Theisen, about his African trip. From now on, "Hemingway" would take precedence over Ernest, inspiring in him a mixture of "almost pathetic" pleasure as well as icy horror: "All this goddam publicity" was Ernest's bitter and pain-filled retort to Hotchner at the beginning of this second African journey.

The Africa that he envisaged as the Promised Land, in which he could embark on another pursuit of happiness, in fact became the theater in which Papa Hemingway offered himself as spectacle. He drank so much that he ended up falling out of his jeep and hurting himself. As he did not sober up during the day, he shot badly and it was so noticeable that even the phlegmatic Percival lost patience. And so, Ernest started to overact. He shaved his head and declared that he wanted to "go native"; he dyed his clothes saffron yellow in imitation of the Massai's robes. For good measure, while Mary was making a round trip to Nairobi, he took a young Wakamba girl named Debba as a lover. On his return to Europe in 1954, he told Hotchner that in September he would have "an African son," but that would always remain in the domain of legend. Mary, who was becoming accustomed to her husband's vain pranks, contented herself with saying that the girl could do with a good wash, but Ernest, for his part, wrote to his New York buddy to boast about his "black and very beautiful" girl who was "absolutely loving and delicate rough," concluding, "Anyway she gives me too bad a hard-on."

Opposite page: A rather cumbersome Ernest boxes a young warrior in shorts, while two others in traditional togas contemplate the scene with a mocking air.

1. Ernest observes a Massai warrior posing with his weapons.

2, 3. Ernest and Mary drive off in a jeep watched by Massai warriors and through Theisen's lens.

4. A young African under the charm of "Papa."

When he abandoned his egocentric, macho role, Ernest rediscovered a little peace of mind. He no longer even shot at the animals but contented himself with watching them or with sitting amid the grandiose landscapes absorbing himself in reading or the peaceful contemplation of nature. To this end, he rented a Cessna to fly over the Murchison Falls, which are the source of the Nile at the end of Lake Victoria. As they flew closer to admire the falls, the pilot was faced with a flock of ibis; to avoid them, he jammed on the controls but got caught in a telegraph cable suspended above the gorge. The pilot then made a forced landing in thicket from which he emerged unscathed, but Mary suffered two broken ribs and Ernest another dislocated shoulder to match the one caused by the jeep accident. The *Herald Tribune* announced Ernest's death, and a jocular pilot named Cartwright "expressed [his] pleasure at finding that the news of his death had been exaggerated," immediately offering to take the Hemingways to Entebbe. A second plane, therefore — and a second crash. No sooner had it begun to bounce down onto the battered runway that the plane caught fire. A man accompanying the Hemingways managed to kick out a window and escape after pushing Mary free of the debris while the pilot did the same. As for Ernest, finding the door stuck, he used his head like a fighting bull to break out of his prison — "all his contradictory wishes to live and die seem to be contained in the terrible, all-out lunges with which he inflicted another concussion on himself." Mary's wounds were painful, but Ernest's nearly killed him. Apart from his serious concussion — as well as blood, cephalian liquid was flowing from his skull — he was wounded in the stomach and the kidneys, seriously enough to kill him twice-over according to the doctors who examined him after a seemingly interminable overland journey.

1, 2. Wreckage of the first plane crash.

3 and opposite page: A visibly reeling Ernest suffering from burns after the second crash.

Announcement of the deaths of Ernest and his wife. The photo is the
one that appeared in *Look*. It is not certain that the leopard was shot
by Ernest, and Mary insisted that this classic image not appear until
her husband had really shot a leopard.

Ernest played the part of "Hemingway" again when he turned up at a press
conference clutching a bottle of gin and a bunch of bananas and declared to the reporters
who had come to see the risen phoenix: "my luck is running good." The character had
found his author. *Newsweek* (from whom *Time* had stolen the limelight by announcing
Hemingway's second death) proclaimed, against all logic and all ethics, that "in defiance
of his doctors' orders" that he should remain in his bed, the indestructible "Papa" had
launched into an ascent of Kilimanjaro. The truth was less glorious and more painful.
Ernest had managed, with great difficulty, to dictate an article about his adventures for
Look; he then went to rest on the coast. A bush fire broke out and, wanting to intervene
at all costs, he managed only to fall into the flames, incurring yet more vicious wounds.

Ernest had entered into his own legend. It was like the story he recounts at the
beginning of *A Moveable Feast*: "The story was writing itself and I was having a hard time
keeping up with it." He would never see Africa again, separated from her by a role that
increasingly escaped him and that others would take a malevolent pleasure in writing for
him. The character would maintain his status, but as Hotchner commented in Venice in
1954, where the Hemingways made a brief stop, Ernest "appeared to have diminished ...
[not] physically diminished, but some of the aura of massiveness seemed to have gone
out of him." "Hemingway" had taken over Ernest.

ISLANDS IN THE STREAM

A Writer Sets Sail

"I had already seen the end of fall come through boyhood, youth and young manhood, and in one place you could write about it better than in another," wrote Ernest, who had always been an observer of nature, from his property of Finca Vigía around 1959. He called the need he experienced all his life to find other places to write "transplanting yourself," adding that it might be as necessary to people as it was to plants.

It was on the advice of John Dos Passos that Ernest and the pregnant Pauline arrived in Key West in 1928. They were returning from their honeymoon and a trip to Spain accompanied, notably, by the painter Waldo Peirce. Key West was a curious place. Situated at the very end of the southernmost territory of the United States, this tiny island of less than 2 by 5 miles (3 by 8 km) was only 95 miles (150 km) from Havana but 125 miles (200 km) from the American continent and almost 1,245 miles (2,000 km) from New York. Today, impressive bridges extend from island to island, allowing one to drive back as far as mile zero on US Highway 1, but at the time of the Hemingways' arrival, the island could be reached only by boat. A minuscule piece of America lost in the middle of the ocean, Key West was "a mixture of Nantucket and New Orleans," with its languorous tropical atmosphere, its cock fighting and its "thriving whorehouses," where, despite Prohibition, alcohol flowed freely. Ernest made one bar, "Sloppy Joe's," particularly famous; its owner, an ex-smuggler of alcohol and Cuban cigars, would become the model for Harry Morgan in *To Have and Have Not*.

Opposite page: Ernest as a young, athletic fisher. Key West, summer 1928.
1. Carlos Gutiérrez (left), original first mate of the *Pilar*, and fishermen.
2. View of Ernest's house from the swimming pool, Key West.
3. Pauline, on the pier of Cojimar. Cuba, 1929.

Ernest hooked up with many characters like Joe, known as "Josie," whose taste for a simple life and rough friendships he shared, without the complications of worldly and literary life. In April 1928, when the local bank refused to cash a check for a thousand dollars for him, it was Joe who took the risk without any form of guarantee. It was also with him that Ernest, who was already an inveterate fisherman, learned the art of tracking marlin. They went on long expeditions together on board Joe's boat *Anita*. After hunting, skiing and bullfighting, Ernest now discovered a new domain of activity that married technique, skill, acquired knowledge, instinct, luck and chance; he was poised to find a new metaphor for writing. The old man's long battle with the marlin in what would become Ernest's emblematic novel was also the struggle of two adversaries who sought to read and outwit each other's strategies. And so the fish takes the old man up to the smooth surface of the sea, out of sight of the land and of his familiar landmarks, just as writing took Ernest to Key West. As always, the writing was to the death: "Fish [...] I love you and respect you very much, But I will kill you dead before this day ends," says the old man.

It was during one of these outings on the *Anita* that Ernest met Carlos Gutiérrez, an expert on marlin and an excellent raconteur of the fishing tales that Ernest adored; Gutiérrez would later become the first mate of the *Pilar*, the emblematic vessel of Hemingway's life in the Caribbean. Ernest rapidly constructed his little world in Key West and incorporated it into his books, such as *To Have and Have Not*, which included numerous friends, lovers and enemies. There were the passing companions such as John Dos Passos and Waldo Peirce but also childhood friends like Bill Smith, the "Bill" of the "Nick Adams" stories and, lastly, several local characters such as "Sloppy Joe" or Charles Thompson, the "Karl" of *Green Hills of Africa*. Ernest created a routine in an environment where Spanish was spoken fluently and where racial mixing was the norm; Europe had indeed wrought changes on the boy from Oak Park.

1. Ernest in Cojimar. Cuba, 1929.
2. End of a fishing trip on board the *Anita*, the boat belonging to "Josie," Ernest's friend.
3. Fine catch, Key West, 1928.
4. John Dos Passos reading to Katy, his wife, on board the *Anita*, 1932.
5. Carlos Gutiérrez and Ernest on board the *Pilar*, around 1934.

H e led a very regulated life that began every day with writing; he would later say, doubtless exaggerating a little, that he had seen the sun rise every day of his life. He sought what he would call "that truth at first light" and developed working habits that would never leave him. For example, he wrote standing up rather than sitting down because, he said, one had more vitality standing: "Who ever went ten rounds sitting on his ass?" He formed the habit of writing narrative passages by hand while he typed dialogue "because people speak like a typewriter works." At half-past three, he left his study in the little extension to the main house and went to 428 Green Street, to Sloppy Joe's, where Skinner, a massively built African-American barman prepared him a long series of drinks, including the most famous, the "Papa doble"; it was also Skinner who, in 1936, would accept a tip of 20 dollars from a pretty blonde, Martha Gellhorn, to be introduced to Hemingway. Ernest drank with his friends, but he was full of energy and basically remained sober. In the Key West period, from 1928 to 1938, he produced many major works, such as *A Farewell to Arms*, *Death in the Afternoon*, *To Have and Have Not* and the African tales, including *Green Hills of Africa*, "The Snows of Kilimanjaro" and "The Short Happy Life of Francis Macomber." "I've ... never felt better or stronger or healthier in the head or body — nor had better confidence of morale — ... since I've been in America," he wrote to his publisher Charles Scribner.

Shortly after their arrival, Ernest's parents came to visit the couple. Ernest found his father thin and tense and was surprised that the latter did not want to deliver Pauline at Petoskey, Michigan. Pauline, therefore, gave birth to Patrick, nicknamed "Mousie," in Kansas City. More traveling ensued. The Hemingways continued their straight diagonal crossing of the United States; from Florida, they went up as far as Wyoming, where Ernest hunted on a ranch belonging to old friends, then Oak Park, then back to Massachusetts, where they met up with Scott and Zelda Fitzgerald again and then finally Key West, at the very south of Florida. On the road — again.

In December, Ernest went up to New York, where he had to collect his first son, Bumby, who was arriving from Paris. On the way, he was intercepted by a telegram that announced, in the laconic and brutal tone typical of this now-defunct mode of communication, that his father had died. Ernest entrusted the task of taking his five-year-old son to his destination to a trustworthy-looking porter and jumped on a train for Illinois. In *Islands in the Stream*, he imagined the telegram announcement of the death of the protagonist Thomas Hudson's wife and children: "YOUR SONS DAVID AND ANDREW KILLED WITH THEIR MOTHER IN MOTOR ACCIDENT NEAR BIARRITZ ATTENDING TO EVERYTHING PENDING YOUR ARRIVAL DEEPEST SYMPATHY." The telegram delivered to Ernest that December 6, 1928, said: "TRY TO LOCATE ERNEST HEMINGWAY IN NEW YORK ADVISE HIM OF DEATH OF HIS FATHER TODAY ASK HIM TO COMMUNICATE WITH HOME IMMEDIATELY." Ernest's father had killed himself with the revolver inherited from his father, Anson, the American Civil War veteran evoked in the memories of Robert Jordan in *For Whom the Bell Tolls*. Ernest, who had seen his father for the last time the previous spring in Key West, was overwhelmed with pain and remorse. He had written to him in December to tell him not to worry and to reassure him, but his letter arrived at 600 North Kenilworth Ave. (or might have arrived, for this was one of Ernest's stories) 20 minutes after the shot had rung out. In 1903, Hadley's father had committed suicide, and she had spoken of it at length to Ernest, who had begun to think that he himself would "go the same way." In June, he christened his son Patrick, thinking that boys should never bear their father's name so as not to have to live up to it, even indirectly.

1. Pauline cuts Ernest's hair on a visit to a friend in Bimini, 1930.

2. Sloppy Joe's bar, run by "Josie," the owner of the *Anita*. The bar is still at the corner of Duval and Green Streets today.

3. On the *Anita*, Ernest and Joe Russell ("Josie") drink to their success. Carlos Gutiérrez is between them, and their friend Joe Lowe is on the right. Key West, 1933.

4. One of the numerous islands in the Gulf Stream where Ernest appreciated the simple, rough lifestyle. He would always be nostalgic for how these landscapes were before the development of mass tourism. Bimini, 1937.

Key West, spring 1928. Clarence and Grace have come to visit Ernest and Pauline, who is pregnant. It would be the last time Ernest saw his father.

1. Ernest's typewriter. He retyped his manuscripts after having reread them dozens of times. Every day of writing began with rereading the pages from the day before.
2. The cemetery for Ernest's cats. These were often polydactyl, having one or two extra claws per paw. The house, now a museum, houses 50 or so of these cats, which the visitor is assured are the descendants of Ernest's own.
3. Ernest's work table in the Finca Vigía, Cuba.

4. Ernest with a fisherman in El Floridita bar, Havana.

5. Ernest was a great lover of cocktails: daiquiris, of course, but also Bloody Marys or else a dry martini. The best martini, he said, was when the Martini stayed behind the bar.

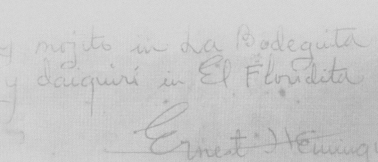

My mojito in La Bodeguita
My daiquirí in El Floridita

Ernest Hemingway

1. Cuban fishers in their boats; these scenes would be reproduced in *The Old Man and the Sea*.
2. Ernest and his sons Patrick ("Mousie") and John ("Bumby") with a beautiful tuna. Bimini, 1935.
3. Ernest and Bumby. Key West, 1928.
4, 5. Ernest and Bumby on board the *Pilar*, 1935. Ernest sometimes amused himself by shooting into the sea and occasionally managed to wound himself with a ricocheting bullet.
6. Traditional pose with the fishing trophies. Hundreds of similar photos of Ernest exist, testament to his talent as a fisherman and to his passion for collecting trophies.

Pauline hoped to give Ernest a daughter, but in 1931 it was a third son, Gregory, who was born. Ernest, who would develop an ambiguous stance to the father-son relationship, nonetheless had a profound influence on the lives of his three boys, seeking to protect them from his blackest and most destructive tendencies but also unable to resist exposing them to the rites and rituals that would make real men out of them. Ernest explored these themes in stories such as "Fathers and Sons" and also in scenes in which sons are called on to show themselves worthy of their fathers' memories and lives — a feeling that Ernest's sons would experience all their lives. In *Islands in the Stream*, they appeared under the transparent mask of altered names: "Tom" was John and "David" was Patrick, Ernest's favorite. In the novel, David struggles with a giant marlin, a fish too big and too heavy for the little boy. The hands and feet of the little David start to bleed, while his big brother anxiously asks the father to stop the deadly game: "I wish the world wasn't the way it is and that things didn't have to happen to brothers." The father, Thomas Hudson, then responds: "I know that if David catches this fish he'll have something inside him for all his life and it will make everything else easier." Not to be a coward, to be a man, a real man. There are things that Ernest would never understand in his life and that only his characters would allow him to see and to express to others — often too late. The novel ends with this sentence: "Oh shit ... you never understand anybody that loves you."

His friend Aaron Hotchner confided that he had received from Ernest a whole philosophy contained in five words: "Never confuse movement with action." This seems paradoxical if one considers Ernest's life: he had returned from his first safari but his life remained a perpetual whirlwind. He went from Florida to Wyoming, passing through Piggott in Arkansas, to the rhythm of hunting and fishing seasons. To this were added the visits to Europe, the ferias of Pamplona, the lightning trips to New York to oversee what was the frenzied literary production of those years. As Thomas Hudson's wife said to him in *Islands in the Stream*, "geography isn't any cure for what's the matter with you." It was when he stopped moving to write that Ernest truly became a nomad, traveling to a yet-to-be-discovered "topography of fiction." He was often in motion, but it was the stationary man who became truly himself, with a pencil or notebook in his hand, as testified by the thousands of written pages as well as his library, which contained some 7,400 books and which he constructed and reconstructed every time he moved house.

Ernest worked a lot at Key West; he also took it easy there. In 1934, he had his own boat built, the *Pilar*, named in honor of the patron saint of the Spanish town of Zaragoza. Continuous fishing expeditions ensued. Ernest had paid for half of this expensive boat with money advanced by *Esquire* for articles the publication had asked him to write — a sign of his fame. In June 1934, President F.D. Roosevelt launched the New Deal, that unprecedented economic revival plan to get America out of the Great Depression. In September, Adolf Hitler became the Führer of Germany, and its army, the Wehrmacht, swore personal obedience to him. Meanwhile, Ernest was fishing or writing articles — "whoring" as his friends reproached him — for the magazine *Fortune*. There were many during that period who felt that Ernest would do better to stop counting and weighing his fish (a compulsive habit he had developed) and involve himself a bit more in the world around him. Although later he would apologize for his excesses, at the time Ernest did not listen to those who upbraided him. He drifted from island to island, from Florida to Cuba, from Cuba to Bimini, that atoll with a primitive way of life that so appealed to him. There, along with the sponge divers and the fishermen struggling to earn a living, loafers, playboys and supposed artists congregated, all trying to forget the world. Ernest, who considered himself the greatest contemporary American writer, was both lauded and denounced. He continually boasted of his exploits and of his physical and moral toughness. He would not tolerate criticism or contradiction, and those who disagreed with him had to face his filthy language or his fists, like the poet Wallace Stevens, with whom he engaged in a memorable bout of fisticuffs in a Key West bar.

He was, however, always capable of transforming his wrath into generous action. He organized, for example, an exhibition in New York for the Spanish artist Luis Quintanilla, whom he had met in Montparnasse in 1922 and who had been imprisoned in his country for engaging in revolutionary activity. Ernest and John Dos Passos were tireless in their efforts and eventually succeeded in releasing the artist, who would later serve as general in the Republican Army during the Spanish Civil War. In 1935 a hurricane hit the islands neighboring Key West, hundreds were affected, mostly the poor and First World War veterans. Ernest wrote an article for the Communist journal *New Masses* in which he denounced the negligence of the authorities, who, although alerted to the imminent catastrophe, had done nothing to protect or shelter the population. Ernest would also demonstrate his generosity with numerous friends and help them financially although his relationship with money always remained somewhat ambivalent. He was very critical about the fortune of his in-laws the Pfeiffers, although it was Uncle Gus who had paid for the safari in Africa; at a time when a meal cost 25 cents, he proposed to invest 800,000 dollars to build bullfighting arenas in Cuba so as to bring tauromachy to the island! In "The Snows of Kilimanjaro," the dying Harry reflects on money's corrupting influence on talent, speaking about his wife's "bloody money," while Thomas Hudson in *Islands in the Stream* talks about his friend Roger, who "has thrown away and abused his talent" by writing to make money. It was a preoccupation that would never leave Ernest. He had always wanted the glory and rewards of success, but he suffered doubt over whether what he produced was indeed the "true" writing that he pursued or simply something used to adorn the lives of the rich and the idle. He would say: "integrity in a writer is like virginity in a woman — once lost, it is never recovered." The image is a brutal one, but it also conveys the fragility of a man who always feared that he would not make the grade.

1. Numerous famous visitors began to gravitate toward the Hemingways. Here we can see the Baron von Blixen (on Ernest's right) and his wife, Eva, beside Pauline. Bimini, 1935.
2. Ernest at his work table, Key West, 1937.
3. Eva von Blixen posing with a fishing trophy. Bimini, 1935.
4. The *Pilar* in her mooring.
5. The Cuban painter Antonio Gatlomo and his wife, Lilian, posing with Ernest and a 130-pound (60 kg) striped marlin caught by Ernest. 1934.

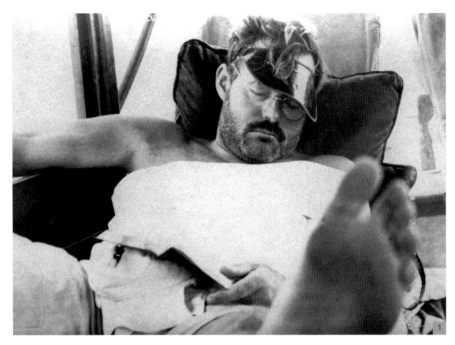

1. Ernest dozing on board the *Pilar* off the coast of Bimini, 1935.
2. Ernest and his friend Joe Lowe; the marlin had been mauled by sharks before being brought aboard.
Opposite page: Ernest's photo collection contained numerous close-ups like this, particularly of fish eyes, a fascination found in *The Old Man and the Sea*.

To Have and Have Not, written in 1937 and his only novel set entirely in America, was Ernest's attempt to respond to those who demanded more commitment and political consciousness from him. The rather moderate success of the novel — both public and critical — showed that it was not here that Ernest exhibited his real conscience but rather in exploring the tensions between men and women or between fathers and sons, thereby saying more about the culture that had created these tensions than speeches denouncing them.

I n 1936, Ernest met Martha Gellhorn. For some time, he had been growing apart from Pauline. He had already in the past "confronted his personal guilt and transformed it into art" in works such as *A Farewell to Arms* or "The Snows." With Martha, Ernest covered the Spanish Civil War; he went back to Pauline from time to time but had already embarked on what was to be another long and painful separation. At the beginning of February 1939, he returned to Key West for a month and lodged at the Hotel Ambos Mundos in Havana, where Martha soon joined him. From April they rented the Finca Vigía, buying it in December; it would be Ernest's principal residence for many years. Ernest began to write *For Whom the Bell Tolls*, which he dedicated to Martha. Later he would say how much he had loved Key West and how well he had worked there, but he also declared, "I'd rather eat monkey manure than die in Key West." In December 1939, he moved the last of his possessions to Cuba. The page had been turned.

While the world was entering into war, Ernest was hunting around Sun Valley, near Ketchum, Idaho. Soon Martha left to report on the conflict in Finland, leaving Ernest feeling "stinko deadly lonely." Afterward, Ernest and Martha, by then married, traveled the length and breadth of Asia, writing about the Sino-Japanese conflict, and then went, each as a correspondent on their own account, to the European front. Ernest had spoken ironically about Martha's desire to spend the honeymoon after their recent marriage on the Burma Road; the relationship broke down and at the end of the war, the couple did not return to the Finca. It was Mary, whom Ernest had met in May 1944 in London, who would now be the muse of the place. The same day that his son John, "Bumby," fell into German hands, Mary came to live in Cuba.

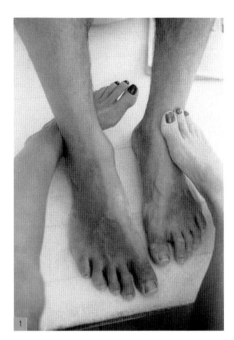

Opposite page: Pauline at the Hotel Ambos Mundos (Both Worlds Hotel), Havana, Cuba, 1928. A stopover during the Hemingways' trip from France to Key West.
1, 2, 3. Ernest and Martha, a new affection and complicity. Finca Vigía, around 1940.

T he Finca would from then on be the place of Ernest's life. It was there that he began all his posthumously published novels — *The Garden of Eden*, *Islands in the Stream*, *A Moveable Feast* and *True at First Light*. The Finca that would be the site of Ernest's disappointment when *Across the River* was rejected by the public and of his triumph with the Nobel Prize, awarded after *The Old Man and the Sea*. The Finca was above all the place where the legend of "Papa" was definitively created. Journalists and reporters from all over the world turned up in Cuba to interview and photograph him from every angle: Papa in El Floridita bar, Papa beside the swimming pool, Papa writing, Papa on the telephone — "They even thought of taking a picture of Blackie [one of his cats] lying in front of my empty chair, just in case," Ernest commented laconically. First flattered by this attention, he soon began to suffer from the constant media attention; just like the money he had courted, the public attention distracted him from his job, which was to write. "Writing at its best is a solitary life," he said to Hotchner and added in a tone reminiscent of Thomas Hudson in *Islands in the Stream*: "He [the writer] sheds off his loneliness and often his work deteriorates."

1. Papa resting, Finca Vigía, 1940.
2. Mary and Ernest with his sister Ursula. Finca Vigía, around 1950.
3. With Spencer Tracy and Gregorio Fuentes during the filming of *The Old Man and the Sea*.
4. Ernest with his portrait, known as "Kid Balzac," painted and inscribed to him by his friend Waldo Peirce at Key West in 1929.
5. Mary reading *The Old Man and the Sea*, Finca Vigía.

Ernest still undertook numerous journeys, to Europe, particularly Spain, and to the United States or on board the *Pilar*, for which Gregorio Fuentes — who would be one of the influences for the character of Santiago in *The Old Man and the Sea* — had become first mate in 1938. And then, of course, there was also the second African safari. Cuba was a home base, but all the media publicity and people distracted Ernest from his work. He could not experience the tranquillity the place could have provided him. He worked on *Islands in the Stream*, with its thinly disguised autobiographical protagonist and events that he no longer sought to transform and transfigure as he had in the past. The book would not be published until 1970, by Mary and his biographer Carlos Baker. "Just as *A Moveable Feast* portrays the most promising part of his life, so *Islands in the Stream* depicts the most depressing." Published nine years after Ernest's suicide and after the biographies that had begun to reveal the architecture of the Hemingway monument, the book underlines the disquiet that inhabits his prose, his dark side and that stream that would eventually carry him off.

1. Ernest on board the *Pilar*.
2. Ernest on the scales; his weight and his blood pressure would be constant preoccupations in the second half of his life. The photo taken by a photographer outside the family circle also shows the growing interest taken by the public in Ernest's private life.
3, 4. Ernest and his cats in Cuba, including "Brie," one of his favorites at Finca Vigía (4).
Right: Ernest the avid reader, here at the Finca Vigía, around 1955.

HE

MING-

WAY

HILLS LIKE WHITE ELEPHANTS

The Lost Eden of Men Without Women

The Lost Eden of Men Without Women

October 1927. After he had divorced Hadley on March 11 and helped her move with their son John into an apartment on the rue Auguste-Blanqui in Paris, Ernest presented her with a new collection of stories, his second, *Men Without Women*. The volume contained 14 stories that all twisted the knife in the still-gaping wound of the alienation, guilt and hope that was, for Ernest, the unchartered territory of a woman. In September 1926, Hadley and Ernest had separated; Hadley had agreed to a divorce on the condition that Ernest wait and see if he was still of the same mind after 100 days without Pauline, the woman with whom he had fallen in love. Their romance had developed quickly after their first meeting in the spring of 1925, during their alpine idyll on the snowy Austrian slopes and the moment when, instead of joining Hadley on his return from New York, he did not take "the first train, or the second or the third" but had remained in Paris with Pauline. On May 10, 1927, they married.

Autumn 1957. Living in Cuba at the Finca Vigía with his fourth wife, Mary, Ernest recorded these moments of crisis in *A Moveable Feast*, which he had just begun, using notes that had been discovered at the Ritz in Paris. The book covers Ernest's youth and ends with the separation from Hadley. Ernest talks about their two last winters in Austria, in Schruns. In 1925, exceptional snowfalls caused avalanches, one of which had killed nine people who had not followed the advice given by the ski instructor of the resort where Hadley, Ernest and their son "Bumby" were staying. Ernest described that terrible "winter of the avalanches" that transformed those who were there into "students" who learned how to recognize the different kinds of snow, avoid the dangerous areas and what to do if they were caught in one. In Ernest's memory, however, that lethal winter was "like a happy and innocent winter in childhood," and nothing, he wrote, "compared to the next winter, a nightmare winter disguised as the greatest fun of all, and the murderous summer that was to follow." The murderous summer and the nightmare winter represented, in Ernest's recollection, the meeting with Pauline and the breakup of his first marriage. The imagery was clear: if Ernest learned to avoid the treachery of the snow cover, he did not succeed in doing so with that equally unstable and dangerous terrain that was his relationship with women.

Avalanches and women were both sources of danger but also sources of writing: "Most of the writing that I did that year was in avalanche time." Ernest wrote out of pain and woundedness, transforming them into art. Thirty years later, he wrote again about this difficult period with its echoes of a paradise lost. For Ernest, love of a woman was bound up with nostalgia or anticipation, rarely with the present, which always escaped him. Women themselves were an inaccessible "other." And so he remembered, "The wool was natural and the fat had not been removed, and the caps and sweaters and long scarves that Hadley knitted from it never became wet in the snow." The women were captured in writing, and the nostalgia of that lost love nestles in the detail of that natural wool and its marvelous qualities that no other material, no other woman, could replace. It should be pointed out that a "restored" version of *A Moveable Feast* appeared in 2009. Edited and prefaced by Pauline's grandsons, Seán and Patrick, this new version diminished the emotional charge connected to Ernest's first divorce and sought to extract Pauline from the bad light in which the book put her.

Opposite page: A matter of measurements: Ernest and his trophy. Sun Valley, Idaho, 1940.
1. Hadley, Ernest's first wife, preparing for her wedding, September 3, 1921.
2, 3. The young suitor, summer 1921.

"When I was young I never wanted to get married," confided Ernest in 1954, "but after I did so, I could never be without a wife again. Same about kids." Numerous stories deal with the emergence from adolescence that commitment to a woman and marriage represented to the adult man. "The End of Something" is one of the first stories on this theme. Nick Adams, Ernest's avatar, breaks off with his girlfriend when everything seemed to unite them because "it isn't fun any more." In 1921, when he was about to get married to Hadley, Ernest wrote to his friend Bill (who appeared in "The End of Something"): "All his life a man loved two or three streams better than anything else in the world. Then, he fell in love with a girl and the goddam streams could dry up for all he cared." Ernest had before him the vision of his father whom he loved and respected but who had been, in his eyes, undone and emasculated by his mother. Ernest would say in his fiction and in numerous conversations that "the big psychic wound of his life had come when he discovered that his father was a coward." He however insisted that no Freudian interpretation should be placed on that — his mother was just, in his own words, "an All-American bitch." Ernest never wrote it explicitly, but he implied many times that his mother had quashed her husband's masculinity and made him into a coward — and becoming a coward was the worst thing that could happen to a man in Ernest's universe — who had ended up committing suicide.

1. Hadley and John ("Bumby"), Ernest's first-born. Paris, 1924.
2. Ernest and "Bumby," the same year.
3. Ernest and Hadley's wedding photo. From left to right, Ursula, Carol (Ernest's sisters), Hadley, Ernest, Grace, Leicester (the Hemingway's youngest child) and Clarence, the father.

During the Parisian years, Hadley was Ernest's discreet companion. Often alone during the day, in society she played the role of the wife. And so, when they visited Gertrude Stein, she talked to Alice Toklas (Gertrude's partner) for, as the latter ironically wrote, it was Alice's function to talk to the wives of the famous men who came to dinner. Stein mocked the stereotyped roles that artists assumed, with the men creating and discussing art while the wives chattered among themselves, discussing mundane trivia. Nonetheless, Paris of the 1920s radically overturned the young Ernest's understanding of life and sexuality. Gertrude Stein's "instruction" about sex made him understand the limits of his simplistic vision of male creator. Ernest expressed his profound disturbance about marriage in numerous stories, such as "Mr. and Mrs. Elliot," in which a writer who cannot conceive a child with his wife also becomes sterile in his writing before having to watch his wife take a woman to her bed instead of him.

It has often been repeated that Ernest was a chauvinist writer who was not interested in women and who celebrated male brutality. However, his male protagonists all show the limits and sterility of the masculine vision of the world. A story like "Cat in the Rain" demonstrates the incomprehension that men in Ernest's universe have for women; when the woman, called only "the American wife," says that she wants to grow her hair, to get a kitten and some new clothes, her husband groans from the bed where he is stretched out with a book: "'Oh, shut up and get something to read.'" Like Hadley at Gertrude Stein's, the anonymous wife is reduced to her marital status, yet all the reader's sympathy goes to the young girl. The man's egotism and immaturity are, far from being celebrated, denounced and condemned in Ernest's story — even if they were not by the real life behavior of "Hemingway."

The other anxiety expressed in this story, as in several others, is that of becoming a father. Beyond the issue of possible conflict with the child, there was the fear that the female partner in the pleasurable sexual game becomes a mother, withdrawing her affection from the man and also, even more importantly, the fear that the child be substituted for artistic energy. The fear that procreation would kill creation. After he married for the second time, to Pauline, they left on a honeymoon to Aigues-Mortes, on the Mediterranean. There he wrote "Hills Like White Elephants," one of Ernest's most moving stories, all the more so as it is narrated from the perspective of the woman. A couple are waiting for a train in the middle of nowhere in Spain; the man is trying to convince his companion to have an abortion so as not to curtail their life of wandering and sexual adventure, as testified by their suitcases and the "labels on them from all the hotels where they had spent nights." The man tries to persuade the woman to do "it" — the word "abortion" is never pronounced — so that they can "have everything" and "go everywhere." When Hadley told Ernest that she was pregnant, he said to Gertrude Stein that he thought he was much too young to become a father. Paternity was seen as the end of freedom and a betrayal.

In the case of Hadley, this betrayal was increased by the incident — trivial in itself but painful in its consequences — of the stolen suitcase containing Ernest's manuscripts. Forty years later, when she was questioned on the subject, Hadley had difficulty holding back her tears. Although Ernest was devastated by the loss of his work, he always assured her that he did not bear her a grudge. However, he drew a mental outline of the world, from which he could not escape, in which the woman was seen as the treacherous destroyer of talent. As Hotchner wrote, for Ernest, "Paris and happiness were synonymous," but that was true only to the extent that Paris was associated in his memory with Hadley as a footloose, childless wife. Although he was quite tender and attentive toward his son, Ernest would always remain convinced that his idealized marriage to Hadley would not have ended if she had not borne a child.

1. "Bumby" in Paris, around 1926.
2. Patrick, known as "Mousie," Key West, 1929.

The Lost Eden of Men Without Women

"This is how Paris was in the early days when we were very poor and very happy." Money was the other betrayal that women would introduce into the life of the man who was a writer. If Hadley was idealized, it was also because she did not have any wealth (even if for a time her allowance ensured the couple's subsistence) and, therefore, represented the artist's ascetic companion for whom "hunger was good discipline." A man's freedom was connected to his poverty — poverty in the very relative sense as experienced by Ernest and Hadley. Pauline, however, was rich. In *A Moveable Feast*, Ernest places the blame for the rupture with Hadley on Pauline and "the rich." Their arrival was announced in a melodramatic and sentimental tone: they "leave everything deader than the roots of any grass Attila's horses' hooves have ever scoured." Pauline was one of the rich, "using the oldest trick there is," who "unrelentingly" comes to steal the husband of the woman who was innocently doing good work beside her writer husband. The good, hard-working and innocent woman, Hadley, was thus undone by the bad woman, Pauline, who is lazy and destructive. In "The Snows of Kilimanjaro," the dying Harry reproaches himself for having married a series of women, each richer than the last, enmeshing him in luxury and leaving him emasculated and emptied of his virile, creative substance. In *A Moveable Feast*, Ernest goes as far as saying that he would have done better to die than to meet the woman who would make him divorce his wife. During his divorce, Ernest willed the rights of *The Sun Also Rises* as well as all ensuing books to "Bumby" (an arrangement that would be modified with ensuing wives and children). In his conflicted relationship with money, Ernest's generosity — he also gave Hadley the Miró painting *The Farm* — was a means of assuaging the remorse and pain he felt.

Opposite page: Pauline, Key West, 1929.

1. Ernest, Pauline and John on the San Sebastian beach.
2. Pauline, in Wyoming in 1932, her dark hair cut in a boy's style; in 1929 (opposite page) she was blonde. Hair was always a subject of fantasy for Ernest.
3. "The dangerous summer" of 1926, in Pamplona. From left to right: the Murphys (friends of the Hemingways), Pauline, Ernest, Hadley and, in front, shoe-shine boys who also want to be in the photo. Everyone seems to be looking elsewhere — or is perhaps already somewhere else.
4. Ernest and Pauline in 1927, the year of their marriage.

153

rnest's consecutive marriages were thus an anguished repetition of the first and an attempt to rediscover that true love of paradise lost. Thirty years later, while he was on safari with Mary, he confided to his "African journal": "The wife I had loved first and best and who was the mother of my oldest son ... tonight, in the dream, I slept happily with my true love in my arms." After the divorce, in story after story and novel after novel, Ernest tried to exorcise his demons of guilt — and like all exorcisms, this one would be violent. During the 100 days of separation between them imposed by Hadley, Ernest wrote to Pauline that he thought of suicide as an escape from the burden of the sin that he was committing because of her. The violence exploded in "Indian Camp," where the father of the child that the doctor, before Nick's bewildered eyes, delivers by cesarean, slits his own throat. In *Islands in the Stream*, Ernest exorcises the violence by killing the protagonist's ex-wife and all their offspring.

A Farewell to Arms is doubtless the most emblematic example of Hemingway's attitude to women. This novel, written during the first years of his marriage with Pauline, depicted the love between Lieutenant Frederick Henry and the nurse Catherine Barkley. After he deserts his unit, bidding farewell to arms, Frederick moves to the pastoral tranquillity of Switzerland. The lovers live happily in a chalet; Catherine is pregnant. But Ernest sacrifices the woman and the child by making them die during childbirth in a Lausanne clinic. One of the first models for Catherine was Agnes von Kurowsky, the nurse with whom Ernest fell in love when he was hospitalized in Milan. The meeting with Agnes was for Ernest the "crowning experience of an extraordinary year." It was the first time he had been truly in love, and the pain was vivid when she threw him over and he had to return alone and distraught to America. However, similar though they were in terms of biographical facts, Agnes represented only a part of Catherine Barkley, who combined, as always with Ernest, several women of his life. Women became accessible to him only when they had been lost to life and were rediscovered in the unknown territory of writing.

1. Ernest and his sons Patrick and Gregory playing with the cats at Finca Vigía, around 1940.
2. Pauline, Key West, 1929.
3. Patrick at Finca Vigía, around 1940.
4. Ernest's three sons, Patrick, John and Gregory, Key West, 1935.
5. John, or "Bumby," posing.

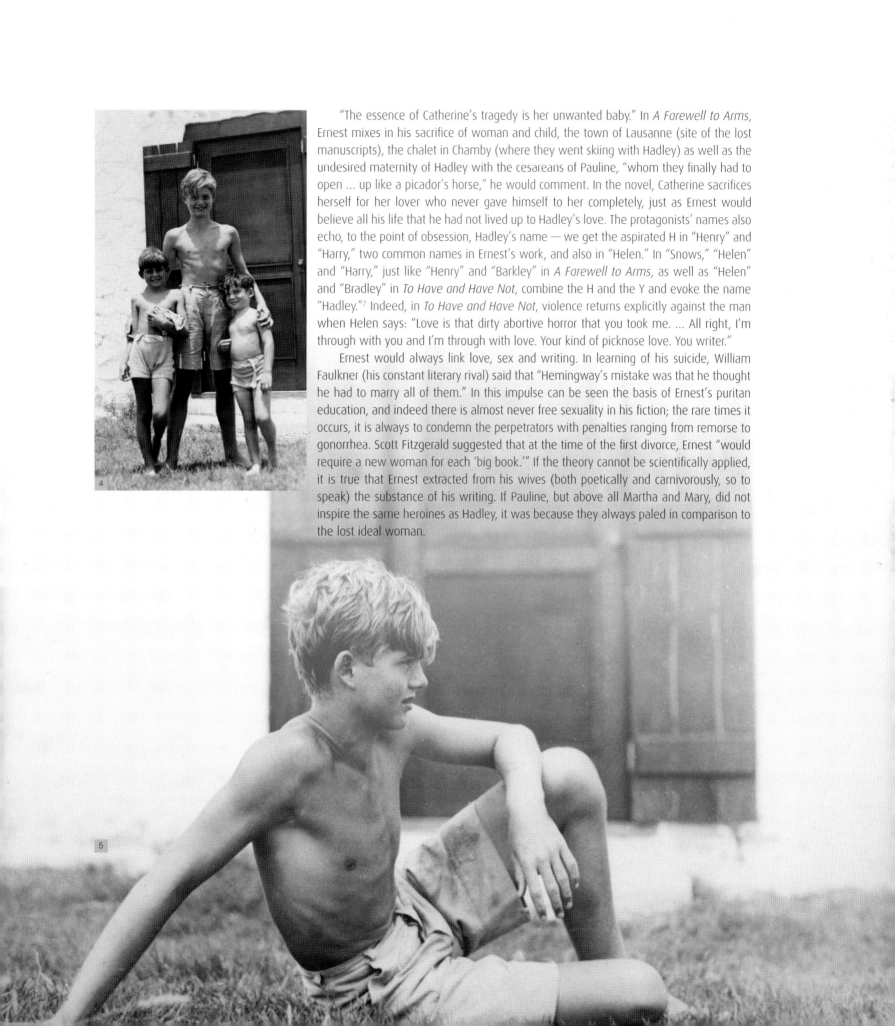

"The essence of Catherine's tragedy is her unwanted baby." In *A Farewell to Arms*, Ernest mixes in his sacrifice of woman and child, the town of Lausanne (site of the lost manuscripts), the chalet in Chamby (where they went skiing with Hadley) as well as the undesired maternity of Hadley with the cesareans of Pauline, "whom they finally had to open ... up like a picador's horse," he would comment. In the novel, Catherine sacrifices herself for her lover who never gave himself to her completely, just as Ernest would believe all his life that he had not lived up to Hadley's love. The protagonists' names also echo, to the point of obsession, Hadley's name — we get the aspirated H in "Henry" and "Harry," two common names in Ernest's work, and also in "Helen." In "Snows," "Helen" and "Harry," just like "Henry" and "Barkley" in *A Farewell to Arms*, as well as "Helen" and "Bradley" in *To Have and Have Not*, combine the H and the Y and evoke the name "Hadley."[7] Indeed, in *To Have and Have Not*, violence returns explicitly against the man when Helen says: "Love is that dirty abortive horror that you took me. ... All right, I'm through with you and I'm through with love. Your kind of picknose love. You writer."

Ernest would always link love, sex and writing. In learning of his suicide, William Faulkner (his constant literary rival) said that "Hemingway's mistake was that he thought he had to marry all of them." In this impulse can be seen the basis of Ernest's puritan education, and indeed there is almost never free sexuality in his fiction; the rare times it occurs, it is always to condemn the perpetrators with penalties ranging from remorse to gonorrhea. Scott Fitzgerald suggested that at the time of the first divorce, Ernest "would require a new woman for each 'big book.'" If the theory cannot be scientifically applied, it is true that Ernest extracted from his wives (both poetically and carnivorously, so to speak) the substance of his writing. If Pauline, but above all Martha and Mary, did not inspire the same heroines as Hadley, it was because they always paled in comparison to the lost ideal woman.

Ernest and Gregory, his third son,
immortalized by Robert Capa in Sun
Valley, Idaho, October 1941.

After finishing a story, Ernest wrote, he "was always empty and both sad and happy, as though I had made love." In the same way, he fulminated: "to interrupt a man while he [is] writing a book ... [is] as bad as to interrupt a man when he [is] in bed making love." Ernest's second divorce would not cause him the same sorrow as the first; he even thought that Pauline had received her just desserts for the harm she had done — "he who lives by the sword dies by the sword!" was his laconic comment. If he divorced Pauline it was also because he had to practice coitus interruptus: because of her two cesareans, Pauline had to avoid getting pregnant again, and her Catholicism meant she would not use contraception. He would regret only one marriage, that to Martha. When after the wedding he went to have a drink and was asked what he wanted, he replied "a glass of hemlock." The marriage to Martha was stormy because they were competitive about everything: Martha was an experienced journalist, was as courageous as a man when she had to write from the frontline and was in no way the docile and attentive sexual partner — all of which meant that Ernest felt challenged as a dominant male in control of his territory. She would be the only wife to leave Ernest and ask for a divorce. Mary, on the other hand, knew how to accommodate the quirks of her famous husband, something that Martha had not known how — or above all wanted — to do. She also knew how to close her eyes to Ernest's dalliances, commenting placidly that like all healthy males, Ernest had to play the field.

Ernest's more or less discreet affairs were always connected to his need to experience fully a sexuality that he felt formed part of his literary expression. One of his most spectacular muses and lovers in the 1930s was Jane Mason, whom the U.S. President Calvin Coolidge would call "the most beautiful woman ever to visit the White House." Jane was very beautiful, but she also had many of the characteristics of Marjorie, that love-struck adolescent in "The End of Something." Jane could drink like a man, adored fishing, adapted to the Spartan conditions on board the *Pilar* and achieved impressive scores at skeet shooting. Sexually active, she had several lovers, which rendered Ernest mad with jealousy; between torrid separations and reunions, Jane would reappear in the guise of the simultaneously attractive and repellent bitch of "The Short Happy Life of Francis Macomber." As was often the case, "the more intense Hemingway's passion was in life, the greater his expression of hatred in his fiction." Jane eventually married a friend of Ernest's, but this encounter was already preparing him for his next relationship — with Martha.

Opposite page: Ernest and Martha, Sun Valley, Idaho, by Robert Capa, 1939.
1. Martha, Finca Vigía, 1940.
2. Ernest, his sons and Martha, in company with Toby Bruce, Ernest's friend and jack-of-all-trades. Sun Valley, 1940.

1. Although he early adopted a tough-guy image, Ernest sometimes appeared dressed as a man of the world. With Mary on board the Île-de-France, en route to Europe, 1949.
2. Venice, 1949.
Opposite page: An Ernest more in keeping with his image, with Mary in Idaho.

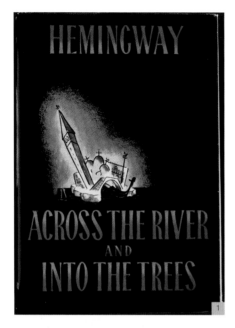

Only two female protagonists escaped Ernest's Anglo-Saxon tendencies, with names sounding reminiscent of Hadley's: Maria in *For Whom the Bell Tolls* and Renata in *Across the River and Into the Trees*. These solar figures were themselves also a combination of women whom Ernest had explored, like so many territories with riches to be appropriated, but they were distinguished above all by the energy and hope that they personified. One of the inspirations for a Hemingway heroine to incite the most comment was that of Renata, the young, beautiful Venetian princess whom Colonel Cantwell would call his "last and only and true love" in *Across the River*. When the relationship between Ernest and Adriana Ivanchich, alias Renata, became public (she would reveal all to the tabloid press), she opined that the valuable role she had played had been "in restoring Ernest's writing vigor." He met Adriana in Italy, where he was traveling with Mary; as she was the same age as he had been when he was wounded at Fossalta, he soon had to include her in the fiction of his life. Ernest and she would become very close, even if, like the colonel's relationship with Renata, his relationship with Adriana remained chaste. Renata assumed her physical and psychological features in the Venetian novel, while the romance of the novel came to compensate Ernest for a love that remained platonic. Adriana would even come to the Finca under Mary's auspices and draw the cover of the first edition of the novel.

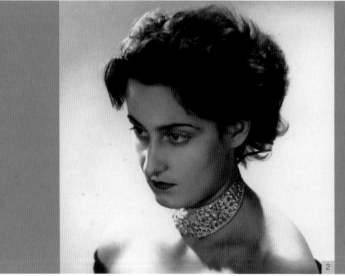

1. The cover of *Across the River and Into the Trees*, drawn by Adriana.
2, 3, 4. Adriana Ivanchich, the beautiful Venetian princess.
Opposite page: Adriana, or the shadow of youth.

Though the novel was badly received by critics at the time (as it still is today), this was partly for the wrong reason. While it is true that the book includes shallow, sentimental passages, it is above all the transparent — almost sincere — identification of Ernest and Adriana that is criticized. Renata (like Maria in *For Whom the Bell Tolls*) offers a vision of youth and rebirth, whereas the other women in his fiction only urge the male protagonist toward the stoic acceptance of decline and death. As he got older, it began to be young women who "sparked the jerky graph of his heart." People wanted the writing to follow the same graph of the heart; if the writing continued, it nonetheless emerged from a man who, for his part, had changed. And the heart of a man is not the same at 50 as it was at 20.

1. Adriana on her visit to Finca Vigía, autumn-winter, 1950–51.
2. Ernest and Lauren Bacall.
Opposite page: Ernest and Adriana, Cuba, 1953.

THE LAST GOOD COUNTRY

Ernest, Hemingway and After

t was an amused Ernest who, having emerged from the savanna after his second plane crash, read the premature obituaries opining that he had succumbed to his long-held desire for death. But, he objected, "[I]f a man sought death all his life, could he not have found her before the age of fifty-four?" In *Across the River*, Colonel Cantwell speaks of his "old brother death," but mostly Ernest talked of it as "that old whore." Death was a familiar companion for Ernest. It had exercised a fascination over him since his earliest childhood, and it had become an integral part of his artistic quest and of his indirect, veiled denunciation of male violence — but it had also become entwined in "Hemingway," the character of his own, sometimes unwitting, creation. And so a sort of self-fulfilling prophecy was created whereby, when his death was announced in 1953, many people saw the news as the confirmation of Hemingway's destiny.

The countless allusions to death in his work and the numerous testimonies of family and friends throughout his life demonstrate his pull toward self-destruction, his desire to turn the world's or his own violence against himself — a violence he recognized but feared he could not assuage by writing. From his adolescence but also during his engagement to Hadley, his relationship with Pauline, his passionate and desperate affair with Jane Mason, his stormy marriage to Martha, his platonic passion for Adriana and in the end the worldwide fame that gave him no respite, Ernest teetered on the edge of the abyss.

When he traveled in the 1950s from Italy to Spain, Ernest was assaulted by a hysterical crowd that threatened to trample him down and that demanded that he "autographed everything from *Of Human Bondage* to *Casserole Cookery*." "Must be the goddamn beard," cried a reeling Ernest, before adding, "I should have stayed in that second kite [plane] in Butiaba." As he said himself, Ernest could no longer take a walk down the road, anywhere in the world, without unleashing a riot. For a man whose trade was writing books, it was an intolerable situation, made all the more so by his overwhelming guilt, acutely conscious as he was that he was partly the source of the problem. "I had a nice private life before ... and now I feel like somebody crapped in it and wiped themselves on slick paper and left it there."

Opposite page: Ernest posing for the bust sculpted by the Italian artist Antonio Lucarda. Torcello, near Venice.

Even though Ernest cultivated an anti-intellectual and antiacademic side, numerous studies appeared about him from the 1950s on. As always, he was flattered by the attention but also irritated when these works did not conform to his own self-image or the image he wanted to project. Although they were of varying quality and gave equally divergent readings of the man and the work, these studies suggest that Ernest was not always the best judge of his work or even of his life. More than anything, Ernest feared psychological and psychoanalytical interpretations of his books, which he considered simply an intrusion into his private life. He knew very well that part of what he wrote was transformed — sometimes before his eyes — into "Hemingway," but more than anything he sought to keep the secret of his fiction's manufacture to himself. If today we know many intimate details about Ernest's life — he rarely bathed, preferring to rub himself with alcohol, disdained underwear, sometimes swore like a trooper, had relationships (consummated or otherwise) with stars ranging from Marlene Dietrich to Ingrid Bergman, taking in Ava Gardner — it is because his private life has become public. His confidant and companion Aaron Hotchner deplored this pillage and blamed Mary, Ernest's literary executor, who contrary to Ernest's express wish had "published a huge volume of ... letters, some of them very, very personal." For her part, Mary declared that if Ernest had known that Hotchner "would one day write a book exposing the paranoid behavior of his last years, he would have killed him — perhaps not ... personally, but seen to it he was disposed of in an automobile accident, say, or out on the Gulf Stream."

Paradoxically, although Ernest seemed constantly to want to impress, he was almost pathologically shy. He abhorred speaking in public, detested fashionable gatherings and was frightened of the telephone — the sole exception being Marlene Dietrich, with whom, although she refused to call him "Papa," he liked to talk on the phone. He was very conscious of his image, playing with it before the camera or on film, yet he liked nothing less than posing — other than for the preestablished ritual frame of fisherman with his catch or hunter with his trophy, the classic compositions that would eventually constitute the visual identity of "Hemingway." The photographer Yousuf Karsh, who took the famous photo of Ernest in a turtleneck sweater, described him as "the shyest man [he] had ever photographed," a man who sought to protect himself behind "a wall of silence and myth." Very unsure of himself, Ernest constantly needed the mirror of others' admiration — a mirror, however, in which he did not recognize himself.

1, 2. With Ingrid Bergman: a lifelong friendship and affection.

3. Hunting party with, left to right, Ernest, Gary Cooper and their guide, Taylor Williams. Idaho, 1940.

Opposite page: When the man and the image become inseparable: portrait of Ernest by Yousuf Karsh, 1957.

Ernest and Marlene Dietrich: he called her "my girl" or, ironically, "the Kraut."
Their love story arose out of a meeting on a transatlantic liner in 1934.
But Ernest believed they were "victims of unsynchronized passion."

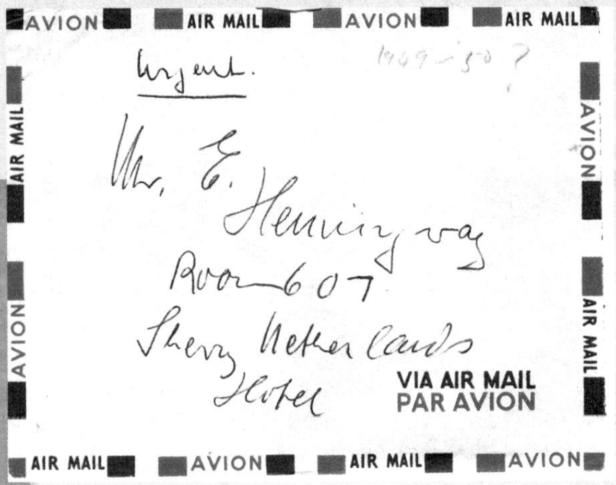

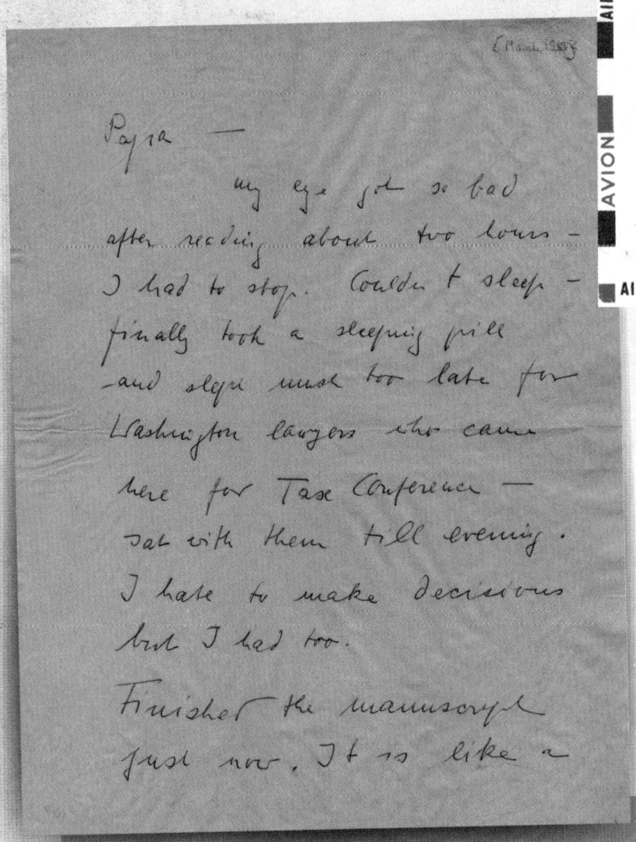

Papa —

my eye got so bad after reading about two hours — I had to stop. Couldn't sleep — finally took a sleeping pill — and slept much too late for Washington lawyers who came here for Tax Conference — sat with them till evening. I hate to make decisions but I had too.

Finished the manuscript just now. It is like a

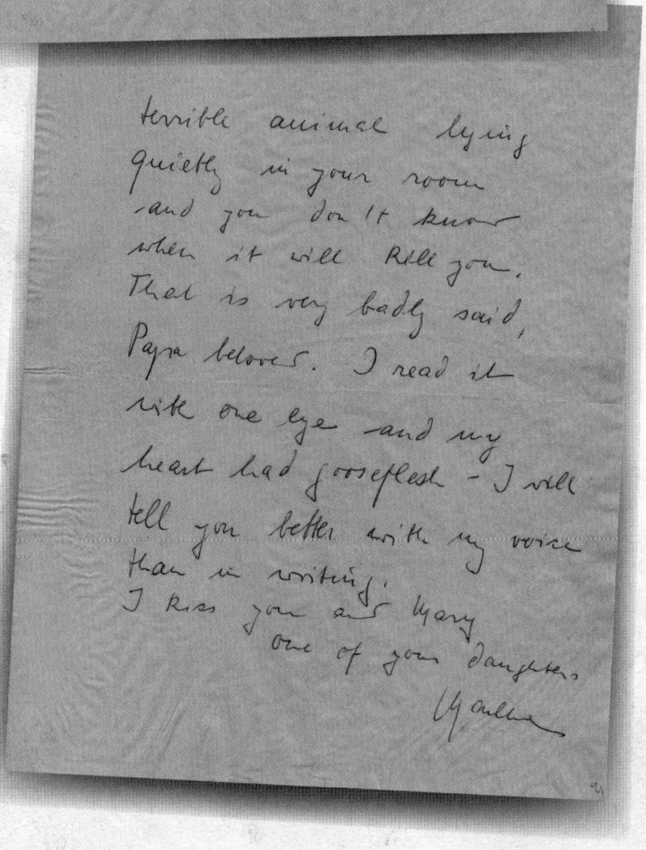

terrible animal lying quietly in your room and you don't know when it will kill you. That is very badly said, Papa beloved. I read it with one eye and my heart had gooseflesh — I will tell you better with my voice than in writing.

I kiss you and Mary

One of your daughters

Marlene

March 1950

Papa —

My eyes got so bad after reading about two hours — I had to stop. Couldn't sleep — finally took a sleeping pill — and slept much too late for Washington lawyers who came here for Tax Conference — sat with them till evening.
I hate to make decisions but I had too.

Finished the manuscript just now. It is like a terrible animal lying quietly in your room and you don't know when it will kill you.

That is very badly said, Papa beloved. I read it with one eye and my heart had gooseflesh — I will tell you better with my voice than in writing.

I kiss you and Mary.

One of your daughters,
Marlene

Your Kraut

The two plane accidents had weakened him, and he increasingly succumbed to alcohol, the professional pitfall of the writer. Although he handled drink well, which generally merely made him a bit more demonstrative and a little less coherent, the testimonies of his sons and those close to him indicate that he downed prodigious quantities. This could mean two or three bottles of strong spirits a day (gin was his favorite) as well as a copious quantity of wine during meals. All this weakened not only his body but also his memory and concentration, without which he could not write. In addition, Ernest was still suffering from the blow of the failure of his last novel — "[I] refuse to read any reviews on *Across the River*, not for blood pressure but they are about as interesting and constructive as reading other people's laundry lists," he said in 1951, the year following the book's publication. The novel, which first appeared as a serial in *Cosmopolitan*, disappointed because it was not equal to *The Sun Also Rises* but also because Colonel Cantwell did not live up to the "Hemingway" legend, which was busily being manufactured by magazines such as *Life*. Ernest no longer managed to write as he wanted and also feared the waning of the "Hemingway" star.

In *Across the River*, the colonel speaks (in French) of the "triste métier" (sad profession) that is war. Hotchner reported that as they were coming back from a drunken evening during which Ernest had talked of the war as a "métier triste [sic]," he said to Hotchner: "You know the real métier triste? ... Writing. There's a real métier triste for you." The remark demonstrates the degree to which writing was a total commitment for Ernest, a question not just of life and death — "writing is the only thing that makes me feel I'm not wasting my time sticking around" — but also of victory and defeat. All his life, he would feel in competition with writers of his time — André Malraux, Sinclair Lewis, Scott Fitzgerald, William Faulkner — and even those of previous centuries: "You should always write your best against dead writers ... and beat them one by one. Why do you want to fight Dostoevsky in your first fight?"

Eleven days after Adriana had left the Finca, on February 17, 1951, Ernest finished *The Old Man and the Sea*. He had put aside *Islands in the Stream*, which he was unable to finish, swept up in the inspiration for writing what he hoped would be his "popular Moby Dick" that would herald his return as champion of the ring. He despaired over the cover of the book, which had the picture of a tuna fish instead of a black marlin, but it did not in any way prevent the book's phenomenal success. Selected as Book of the Month, ensuring a first print run of 153,000 copies, on September 1 it was featured in *Life* and 5,300,000 copies of the magazine were sold. Following Scribner's print run of the first 50,000 copies, some hundred thousand dollars in rights, in the first year, were sold for foreign translations. It is hard to assess the quality of the book amid such a media frenzy and whirlwind of figures. Yet it can safely be said that *The Old Man and the Sea* is not a book without faults. There are sentimental passages reminiscent of the least successful passages of *Across the River*, platitudes served up in the guise of philosophical profundities and also the heavy Christian symbolism that the film (mediocre and despised by Ernest) only accentuated. But Hemingway had become an irresistible force; he had succeeded in making a comeback.

Opposite page: Ernest with the actor and playwright Noel Coward at Sloppy Joe's, during the filming of Carol Reed's *Our Man in Havana*.

1. Cover of *Life*, September 1952, the edition that published *The Old Man and the Sea*.
2. When a writer is one of the most famous men on earth ...

Photos from films that would make Hemingway part of the 20th century collective imagination, as a figure of both academic and popular culture:

3. Henry King's *The Snows of Kilimanjaro* with Gregory Peck, Ava Gardner and Susan Hayward.
4. *A Farewell to Arms* with Rock Hudson.
5. *For Whom the Bell Tolls* with Gary Cooper and Ingrid Bergman.
6. *The Old Man and the Sea* with Spencer Tracy.

GREGORY PECK in **Schnee am KILIMANDSCHARO**
SUSAN HAYWARD · AVA GARDNER · HILDEGARD KNEF

3

GARY COOPER
INGRID BERGMANN
AKIM TAMIROFF

in

„Wem die Stunde schlägt"
(FOR WHOM THE BELL TOLLS)

Regie: SAM WOOD

Ein Farbfilm

Ein Film der Paramount · Im Verleih der Universal

5

4

6

SPENCER TRACY
in
ERNEST HEMINGWAY's

**DER ALTE MANN
UND DAS MEER**
(THE OLD MAN AND THE SEA)

Regie: John Sturges

Ein Farbfilm in
WarnerColor

rnest had also aged prematurely when he came back from Africa in 1954. He was only 55 but looked 10 years older. His hair had whitened and thinned out all at once, while his walk, which had always been impressively confident, had become faltering. He had already received the Pulitzer for *The Old Man* and rather than being able to relax on his return from Africa, he was predicted to win the Nobel Prize; the pressure began to mount again. In his state, he was "in no shape for this tougher Prize-combat," which was nonetheless awarded to him that autumn. Declaring himself too ill — but above all wanting to avoid all the social hullabaloo — he refused to go to Sweden and asked the American ambassador to read a short and lucid acceptance speech: "Writing, at its best, is a lonely life. ... He grows in public stature as he sheds his loneliness and often his work deteriorates."

The following summers, spent mainly in Cuba, would be among the least active of Ernest's life, preoccupied as he was in fighting all sorts of illness and wounds. It was another paradox of this man who appeared so tough and strong that he was in fact physically fragile. Since adolescence, his life had been a series of more or less serious pains and injuries as well as ailments aggravated by his heavy drinking. One after the other, doctors tried to get him to adopt a lifestyle more in keeping with the state of his health. Instead, Ernest embarked on a vicious circle in which, falling ill from his blood pressure and high cholesterol, he would go on a diet; oppressed by this monastic regime, he would start drinking again, and round it would go.

1. Ernest and Fidel Castro: the most famous bearded men of the 1950s.
2. A delighted Ernest studies his Nobel Prize, 1954.
3. Hemingway becomes a brand. In Pamplona, as in Madrid, Paris or Key West, a place was advertised by declaring that "Papa" had frequented it. A restaurant in Madrid still displays a mocking notice stating: "We guarantee that Hemingway never ate here."
4. Every two years, the Hemingway Society Conference gathers specialists and aficionados from all over the world around the figure of Papa. Here it is being held in Lausanne, July 2010.
5. The Papa Look-alike Contest, held every year in Key West.
6. Life-size bronze statue of Hemingway in El Floridita bar, Havana.

Toward the end of the 1950s, Cuba started to weigh on Ernest; it was no longer a haven but an anxiety-ridden hideout where life had caught up with him. He was a celebrity, and he was much solicited to give publicity to Batista's government. He could not go out of his house without hearing people calling him: "Papa! Papa!" People no longer went to "El Floridita" to have a drink but in the hope of seeing Ernest, or rather "Hemingway," propped up at the bar. The tropical heat became difficult for the ill man that he was. Hurricanes ravaged the island, and Ernest despaired over the damage inflicted to the landscape by the storms but above all by the development of tourism. The heavy meteorological climate reflected the political one: the corrupted Batista regime had its back against the wall, and a new, political hurricane was about to sweep through the island.

His nostalgia for his emotional support of the leftist Spanish during the civil war, his lack of participation in the violence of the Cuban revolution and, finally, the fact that his property had been spared by the fighting all caused Ernest to welcome the new Castro regime with reconciliatory good will. In the climate of strong anti-Americanism that reigned on the island, Ernest, who had always hated Batista's cruelty, remained popular. "Sic transit hijo de puta" (so passes a son of a bitch) was his epitaph for Batista while he entered into friendly relations with a Fidel Castro only too happy to appear with a gringo who had ostensibly been won over to the revolutionary cause. A Soviet minister even visited the Finca and offered to pay Ernest the royalties that the USSR had frozen; Ernest refused unless they also be granted to other American writers. The situation continued to deteriorate: soon his friends were expropriated and exiled by the regime. The gap widened between Ernest the writer and friend and Hemingway the public figure whom the regime wanted to use to its own advantage.

In 1958 he returned to Ketchum in Idaho. He renewed his friendship with Gary Cooper, the actor in *For Whom the Bell Tolls* and *A Farewell to Arms*, and hunted with him in Sun Valley. In 1959, he was in Spain, where, on behalf of *Life*, he followed the *mano a mano* between Domínguín and Ordóñez with a renewed passion for the bullfight. Bullfights and the hills of Idaho: this was the landscape of his youth.

Opposite page, 1: Ernest opens presents and telegrams of congratulations at La Consula (Andalucía) on the occasion of his 60th birthday.

2. "Nothing changes a friend as much as success, whether ours or his." A premonitory dictum written on the wall of Ordóñez's ranch.

I n his 60th year, Ernest needed a new horizon; he and Mary started looking for a new permanent base outside Cuba. As in that late Nick Adams story, written in the 1950s, "The Last Good Country," he had to cross over the terrifying swamps of reality to get to a new "secret place." For Ernest, "elsewhere" was always more beautiful.

Ernest's 60th birthday was the occasion for a memorable party at an estate, La Consula, in the south of Spain. As it coincided with the birthday of Carmen Ordóñez, the matador's wife, a huge fiesta was organized to celebrate the great man — who, it was clear, was in decline. From his own admission, Ernest had always presented himself as a brawler, a pain in the neck, intrusive, "an irritating son of a bitch," but from now on his values had changed. The man who had always handled guns with respect and caution now amused himself shooting cigarettes out of guests' mouths or, having always defended the ethic and purity of bullfighting, now got his pal "Hotch" to dress up as a matador and had him parade in the paseo of Ordóñez. He had always respected manly friendship but now lost his temper when jostled by his friend and companion in arms, C.T. Lanham, who came specially to see him, crying "that no-one was allowed to touch his head." Nothing was refused the *figura*, the great celebrity, but testimonies abounded as to the disturbing and frightening outbursts and ensuing bouts of depression.

The scenario had become a familiar one: each time that a place became too cramped or hostile for him, Ernest overdid things, thrashed about and started to look for a new "elsewhere." So he tried Spain again: bulls, writing and death. A new romantic passion as well, much to the displeasure of Mary, who as with the episode with Adriana, again had to swallow her jealousy and her pain — Ernest was cruel in his passions and one did not argue with Hemingway. She was young, intelligent and lively, very pretty of course, with her freckles and her mixture of reserve and that boldness that belongs to youth that has nothing to lose. In Ernest's imagination, Valerie Danby-Smith had "a vague resemblance to some of the pale noble ladies painted by Goya," and he managed to keep her around him by engaging her as a very personal assistant. Opinions differ as to the degree of intimacy between them, but, whatever the case, Ernest forged a very strong tie with Valerie, in a relationship that he perhaps hoped would give him renewed emotional and creative force.[8]

Back in Cuba, Ernest finished *The Dangerous Summer* on May 28, 1960, and worked on *A Moveable Feast*. When the book appeared three years after his death, it became the reference point by which his whole body of work was judged. However, more than an autobiography, *A Moveable Feast* was a fictional work in which Ernest portrayed in his own way the emergence of Hemingway. Only months before being admitted to the Mayo Clinic to undergo psychiatric electroconvulsive shock treatment, Ernest demonstrated that he was once again capable of producing powerful writing — even if the literal truth of events had to suffer in the process.

Meanwhile, Castro had nationalized all private property in Cuba. Ernest was not very attached to possessions, but he cared about his manuscripts and his paintings. When Hotchner and he tried to go to New York to give Scribner's the manuscript of *The Dangerous Summer*, Castro prevented them by canceling all flights to the United States. An old smuggling pal of Ernest's took Hotchner with the pile of typewritten papers to Key West in a Cessna "without benefit of the Havana customs." Ernest and Mary eventually arrived in New York, where Ernest, Hotchner and Scribner discussed which manuscript to publish first, as if time was limited.

1. View from a window at Ketchum, Ernest's last home.
2. Ernest, Idaho, 1960. The photographer, John Bryson, told him he wanted a photo with action.
Opposite page: Idaho, 1960.

Ernest's health was bad. As well as the ailments that had afflicted him all his life, he suffered from depression and paranoia and manifested suicidal tendencies. In November 1960, he went into a deep crisis that left his friends and family feeling helpless. Mary hoped that the Ketchum hills, which reminded Ernest of Spain, would comfort and calm him, but he remained agitated, refusing to go hunting with his friends or going with great unwillingness. Hotchner came to join him there, but while he tried to cheer him up with news of the Hollywood project for an adaptation of the Nick Adams stories with Gary Cooper in the title role, Ernest raged that his telephone was being bugged and that he was being shadowed by FBI agents. Depressed at the loss of the Finca, which had been nationalized by the Cuban revolution, and unable to concentrate on revising his manuscripts, Ernest "would sometimes stand at the gun rack of rifles, holding one of the guns, staring out of the window at the distant mountains."

The psychiatrist contacted by Hotchner in New York described "Ernest's general condition as depression-persecutory." On November 30, he had him admitted under the name of a close friend to the Mayo Clinic in Rochester, Minnesota. In December, Ernest received 11 electroconvulsive shocks that served only to increase his suffering, physically and particularly psychologically. The doctors considered that he had responded well to treatment, but Mary, abandoned during that Christmas period, saw her husband deteriorating before her eyes. "What these shock doctors don't know is about writers and such things as remorse and contrition and what they do with them," said Ernest to Hotchner, "what is the sense of ruining my head and erasing my memory, which is my capital, and putting me out of business?"

A few days after this conversation with Hotchner, on January 22, 1961, Ernest left the clinic. Back in Ketchum, he returned to hunting, talked about projects, took renewed interest in the Hollywood adaptation of "The World of Nick Adams." But in April he despaired of finishing *A Moveable Feast*, which he had promised Scribner's: "This wonderful damn book, I can't finish it. ... Not this fall or next spring or in ten years from now. I can't."

Ernest tried to throw himself into an airplane propeller turning on the runway; he talked about suicide more and more often. Eventually he agreed to a second hospitalization in Rochester. He received more electroconvulsive shocks, which he protested were destroying his memory. The doctor in charge of Ernest recited a long list of mental problems — hallucinations, persecution complex, paranoia, anxieties — as if he were saying a rosary: a rosary that would serve in an exorcism rather than a prayer.

1. With Gary Cooper. Ernest loved the actor because he was "true to his own identity." He was devastated to learn that Cooper was suffering from cancer, which would kill him a few weeks before his own death.
2. Religious ceremony at Ernest's burial, Ketchum, Idaho.

I n *To Have and Have Not*, a character contemplates a Colt gun and speaks of "those admirable American instruments so easily carried, so sure of effect, so well designed to end the American dream when it becomes a nightmare, their only drawback is the mess they leave for relatives to clean up." On July 2, Mary heard what sounded like two drawers slamming shut. Friends would come to clean everything up so that the sitting room in which Ernest had put two bullets in his head bore "no sign of disorder or stain." The strictly private burial in Ketchum was the site of what were already tensions between those who laid claim to the memory and inheritance of "Papa." Ernest once said: "Old as I am, I continue to be amazed at the sudden emergence of daffodils and of stories."

As are the continuing generations of his readers.

1899

July 21
Birth of Ernest Miller Hemingway in Oak Park, Illinois.

1900
Clarence and Grace Hemingway have a chalet built beside Lake Walloon; the chalet will become "Windemere."

1909
Ernest's father gives him his first hunting rifle.
African safari of Theodore Roosevelt, Ernest's role model.

1912
Ernest composes his first poem.

1913–1916
Attends Oak Park High School.

1917
Ernest becomes a reporter for the *Kansas City Star*.

1918
April
Ernest volunteers for the Italian Red Cross.

May 23
Crosses the Atlantic on board the *Chicago*.

July 8
At Fossalta di Piave, Ernest's legs are seriously wounded. He is hospitalized near Milan, where he meets Agnes von Kurowsky.

1919
January
A vexed Ernest returns to the United States.

1920
January–May
Stay in Toronto, Canada.

1921

September 3
Ernest marries Hadley Richardson.

December 22
The couple arrives in Paris.

1922
March
Meeting with Gertrude Stein.

September
Ernest sent to Turkey, where he covers the Greco-Turkish War for the *Star*.

December
Peace conference in Lausanne.

1923
June
First trip to Pamplona.

August
Ernest's first book, *Three Stories and Ten Poems*, printed in Dijon.

October 10
Birth of John Hadley Nicanor Hemingway, nicknamed "Bumby."

1924
January 19
Ernest and Hadley move into 113 rue Notre-Dame-des-Champs in Paris.

September
Ernest, Hadley and Bumby spend the winter in Schruns, in Vorarlberg, Austria.

1925
May
Start of friendship with Francis Scott Fitzgerald.

October
Publication in New York of *In Our Time* (Boni & Liveright). Ernest acquires Miró's *The Farm*, which he gives to Hadley.

Opposite page:
Pocket watches belonging to Ernest.

December 25
Pauline Pfeiffer joins the couple in Schruns.

1926

March
Ernest begins an affair with Pauline Pfeiffer in Paris.

May
Publication of *The Torrents of Spring* (Scribner's).

October 22
The Sun Also Rises published by Scribner's.

1927

March 11
Ernest and Hadley divorce.

May 10
Ernest marries Pauline Pfeiffer.

1928

March
Ernest and Pauline move to Key West.

June 27
Birth of Patrick "Mousie" Hemingway.

December 6
Clarence Hemingway commits suicide by shooting himself in the head.

1929

September 27
Publication of *A Farewell to Arms*.

1931

November 12
Birth of Gregory Hancock Hemingway, nicknamed "Gigi."

1932

September 23
Publication of *Death in the Afternoon*.

1933

December
Arrives in Africa for the first African safari, led by Philip Percival.

1934

May
Ernest takes delivery of his boat, *Pilar*.

1935

October 25
Publication of *Green Hills of Africa*.

1936

August
"The Snows of Kilimanjaro" published in *Esquire*.

1937

January
Ernest is a war correspondent in Spain with the North American Newspaper Alliance.

March
Arrival in Barcelona; collaboration with Joris Ivens for the film *The Spanish Earth*.

July 8
Meeting in Key West with Martha Gellhorn, who has come to interview him.

September
Ernest and Martha go to Madrid.

October 15
Publication of *To Have and Have Not*.

1939

April
Martha rents Finca Vigía in Havana.

1940

October
Publication of *For Whom the Bell Tolls* (dedicated to Martha).

November 21
Ernest marries Martha Gellhorn in New York.

1941

February–March
Voyage to China with Martha, who is covering the Second Sino-Japanese War.

Opposite page:
Ernest's portrait, also known as "Kid Balzac," by Waldo Peirce, 1927.

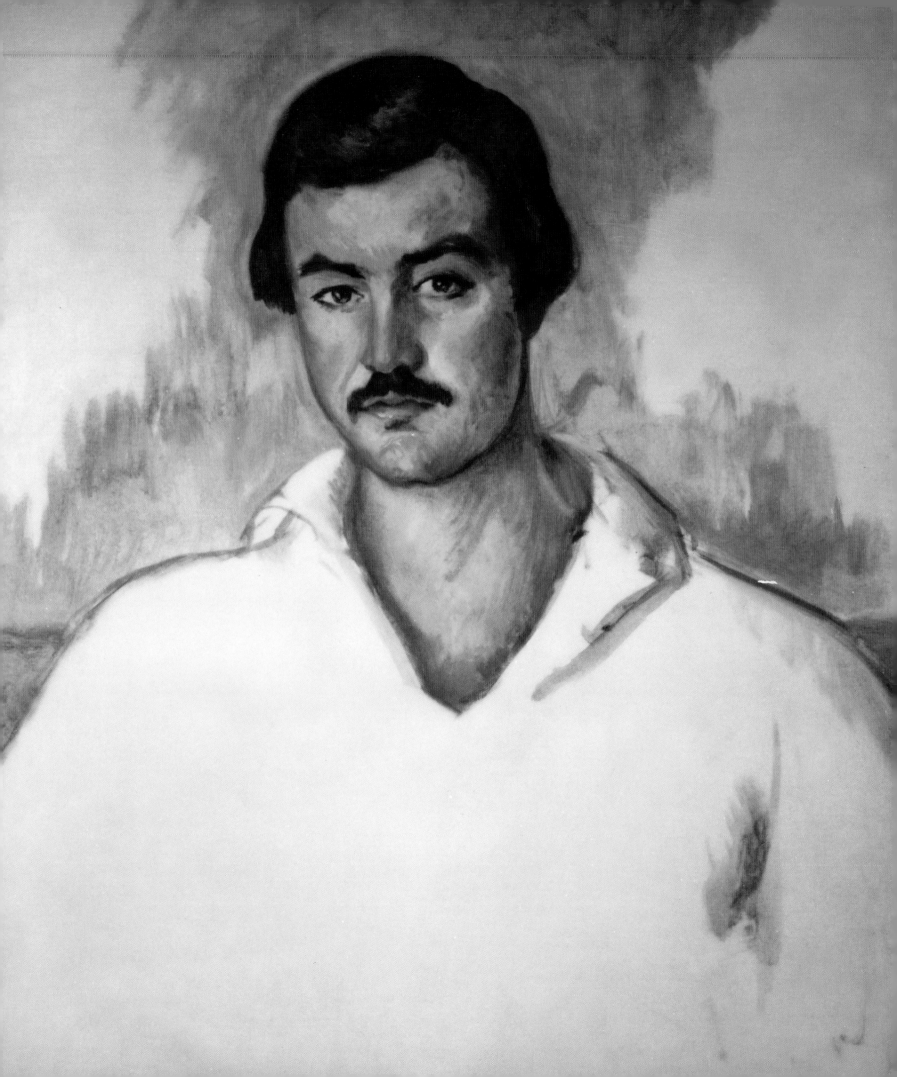

1942

June

Counterespionage on board *Pilar*, tracking German submarines.

1944

March

Trip to Europe with Martha to cover the war for *Collier's*.

May 17

Ernest meets Mary Welsh in London.

August 25

Ernest enters Paris with the F.F.I. (French Forces of the Interior).

October 27

Ernest learns that his son John has been taken prisoner by the Germans.

December

Ernest joins the Lanham regiment in the Ardennes after the German counteroffensive.

1945

May 2

Mary arrives at Finca Vigía.

1946

March 14

Ernest marries Mary Welsh in Havana.

1948

December

Meeting with Adriana Ivancich.

1950

September

Publication of *Across the River and Into the Trees*, for which Adriana draws the cover.

1951

June 28

Death of Grace Hemingway in Memphis.

September

Death of Pauline in Los Angeles.

1952

March

Coup d'état by Batista in Cuba.

September

Publication of *The Old Man and the Sea* in *Life* magazine.

1953

May

Pulitzer Prize for *The Old Man and the Sea*.

August

Departure for the second African safari, again accompanied by Philip Percival.

1954

February

Ernest's plane accidents are reported in national newspapers after the erroneous announcement of his death.

October 28

Announcement of Ernest's Nobel Prize for Literature.

1958

October

Move to Ketchum, Idaho.

1959

May

Trip to Spain, where Ernest attends the corridas of brothers-in-law Dominguín and Ordóñez.

1960

July

Ernest leaves Fidel Castro's Cuba for good.

September

Last trip to Spain. On his return, Ernest is hospitalized at the Mayo Clinic in Rochester, Minnesota.

1961

April–June

Another hospitalization at the Mayo Clinic, where he undergoes electroconvulsive therapy. He then returns to Ketchum by car.

July 2

Ernest Hemingway commits suicide with his rifle.

Opposite page:
Cuban fishermen in 1934.

P. 32 [1] I am indebted to Kenneth Lynn for this connection between Hemingway's life and Walpole's fiction.

P. 70 [2] A Moveable Feast, a posthumous memoir, was published in 1964 by Scribner's in New York. Ernest worked on it during the last years of his life in Cuba, and it was completed by Mary, Ernest's last wife; to this day, it remains uncertain what was contributed by Ernest and what by Mary. A new version edited by Seán Hemingway, Ernest's grandson with his second wife, Pauline, was published in 2009. This new edition sought to correct the negative image given of Pauline in the 1964 version in which Hadley, the first wife, was presented as the source of a happiness that would never return after Ernest left her. See chapters 7 and 8.

P. 86 [3] A bullfight with young bulls.

P. 86 [4] Original Spanish text: "España es el único país donde la muerte es el espectáculo nacional."

P. 105 [5] Hans Meyer, Across East African Glaciers: An Account of the First Ascent of Kilimanjaro (London, 1891). On the first maps of Tanganyika, one of the three peaks that form the summit of Kilimanjaro bore the name of this geologist, who attained the summit, after three attempts, in 1889.

P. 109 [6] The phrase "theater of masculinity" refers to the title of the book by Thomas Strychacz, Hemingway's Theaters of Masculinity (Louisiana State University Press, 2003).

P. 155 [7] I am indebted to Jeffrey Meyers for drawing my attention to this passage of To Have and Have Not and for the astute observation about the names of Hemingway's protagonists [Meyers, 294–95].

P. 181 [8] Valerie Danby-Smith is known by the name of Valerie Hemingway, a name she took on her marriage to Gregory (the third son, born to Pauline). Valerie would meet Gregory at Ernest's funeral in 1961 and, as she writes in Running with the Bulls [RWB, 106], led a turbulent, frightening, marvelous and sensational life with him before their divorce, Gregory's sex change and finally his death in tragic circumstances.

Opposite page:
Safari, 1953, by Theisen.

BAKER, Carlos. *Ernest Hemingway: A Life Story*. New York: Charles Scribner's Sons, 1969. [Baker]

BATAILLE, Georges. *Les larmes d'Éros*. Paris: Jean-Jacques Pauvert, 1961, and 10/18, 1971. (Translation in text by Catherine Spencer.) [Bataille]

DONALDSON, Scott. *By Force of Will: The Life and Art of Ernest Hemingway*. New York: The Viking Press, 1977. [Donaldson]

DUPUY, Pierre. *Hemingway et l'Espagne*. Tournai, Belgium: La Renaissance du Livre, 2001. [Dupuy]

GARCÍA LORCA, Federico. "Teoría y juego del duende." In *Obras complétas*, vol. 3, Edición de Miguel García-Posada. Madrid: Opera Mundi/Galaxia Gutenberg. [Lorca]

GARY, Romain. *Éducation européenne. In Légende du je*. Paris: Mireille Sacotte, 1956, and Paris: Gallimard/Quarto, 2009. (Translation in text by Catherine Spencer.) [Gary]

GRIFFIN, Peter. *Along with Youth; Hemingway: The Early Years*. New York and Oxford: Oxford University Press, 1985. [Griffin]

HEMINGWAY, Ernest. *Across the River and Into the Trees*. New York: Charles Scribner's Sons, 1950. [ARIT]

HEMINGWAY, Ernest. *The Complete Short Stories of Ernest Hemingway: The Finca Vigía Edition*. New York: Charles Scribner's Sons, 2003. [CSS]

HEMINGWAY, Ernest. *The Dangerous Summer*. New York: Touchstone, 1997. [DS]

HEMINGWAY, Ernest. *Death in the Afternoon*. New York: Charles Scribner's Sons, 1932. [DIA]

HEMINGWAY, Ernest. *A Farewell to Arms*. New York: Charles Scribner's Sons, 1929. [FTA]

HEMINGWAY, Ernest. *For Whom the Bell Tolls*. London: Arrow Books, 1994. [FWTBT]

HEMINGWAY, Ernest. *Green Hills of Africa*. London: Arrow Books, 1994. [GHA]

HEMINGWAY, Ernest. I*slands in the Stream*. New York: Charles Scribner's Sons, 1970. [IS]

HEMINGWAY, Ernest. *A Moveable Feast: The Restored Edition*. Edited by Seán Hemingway. New York: Charles Scribner's Sons, 2009. [MFRE]

HEMINGWAY, Ernest. *The Old Man and the Sea*. New York: Charles Scribner's Sons, 1952. [OMS]

HEMINGWAY, Ernest. *The Sun Also Rises*. London: Arrow Books, 1994. [SAR]

HEMINGWAY, Ernest. *To Have and Have Not*. New York: Charles Scribner's Sons, 1937 (reprint, 1996). [HHN]

HEMINGWAY, Valerie. *Running with the Bulls: My Life with the Hemingways*. New York: Random House, 2004. [RWB]

HOTCHNER, Aaron E. *Papa Hemingway: A Personal Memoir*. New York: Da Capo Press, 1966 (reprint, 2005). [Hotchner]

KERT, Bernice. *The Hemingway Women*. New York: W.W. Norton & Company, 1983. [Kert]

LEIRIS, Michel. "De la littérature considérée comme une tauromachie." In *L'Âge d'homme*, Gallimard, Paris, 1939, and Gallimard/Folio, 2006. [Leiris]

LYNN, Kenneth. *Hemingway*. New York: Simon & Schuster, 1987. [Lynn]

MEYERS, Jeffrey. *Hemingway: A Biography*. London: Macmillan, 1985. [Meyers]

REYNOLDS, Michael S. *Hemingway's First War: The Making of A Farewell to Arms*. New Jersey: Princeton University Press, 1976. [Reynolds]

STEIN, Gertrude. *The Autobiography of Alice B. Toklas*. New York: Library of America, 1998. [STEIN]

INTRODUCTION

p. 11: "cherished the hope that Ernest's hair would remain blond" [Lynn, 42]; "Edenic infancy" [Lynn, 43].

CHAPTER 1

p. 21: "Prose is architecture, not interior decoration, and the Baroque is over" [DIA, 191]. p. 23: "that bitch" [Kert, 21]; "the dark queen of Hemingway's inner world" [Lynn, 65]. p. 24: "my precious boy, a 'real' boy" [Lynn, 65]. p. 25: "was as sound [on hunting and fishing] as he was unsound on sex" [CSS, 370]. p. 30: "a relief to them both to escape into a world of men without women" [Lynn, 62]. p. 31: "The sweet smile on his face masked the savagery in his heart" [Lynn, 60]. p. 32: "big words" [Hotchner, 70]. p. 35: "I was an awful dope ... I can remember thinking that we were the home team and the Austrians the visiting team" [Baker, 38]; "for all his patriotism" "the prospect of trench warfare" [Lynn, 73]; "felt quite sure he would never die" [CSS, 70].

CHAPTER 2

p. 39: "geographical descriptions were indeed painfully conscious" [Baker, 13]; "This is the first time my country ever fought that I was not there, and food has no taste, and the hell with love when you can't have children" [Hotchner, 69]; "the geography is perfectly accurate" [Reynolds, 5]. p. 40: "one becomes so accustomed to the sight of all the dead being men that the sight of a dead woman is quite shocking" [CSS, 336]; "the human body blown into pieces which exploded along no anatomical lines" [CSS, 337]; "I am going to get out of this ambulance section and see if I can't find where the war is" [Baker, 43]. p. 42: "Hun theory that nothing takes a soldier out faster than to have his balls shot off" [Hotchner, 48]; "227" [Hotchner, 103]; "in a flash, as when a blast-furnace door is swung open" [FTA, 54]. p. 43: "have some fun at the expense of gullible civilians" [Donaldson, 139]; "[t]he taking of Paris was nothing, ... only an emotional experience" [ARIT, 98]; "magnificent in the war but insufferable in peace" [Donaldson, 143]. p. 47: "called for a Goya" [DIA, 134]; "call for pictorial representation in their plight but ... call for someone to alleviate their condition" [DIA, 135]; "Of all the ways to be wounded. I suppose it was funny" [SAR, 26]; "greatest of outdoor sports" [Meyers, 398]; "having conquered his fears, he took a hard line towards those who could not cast off their own" [Donaldson, 134]; "[H]e was a cobarde. Go on, say it in English. Coward. ... He was just a coward and that was the worst luck any man could have" [FWTBT, 361]. p. 51: "I hope to go to Spain if it isn't all over" [Dupuy, 264]. p. 52: "[Y]ou have not been a professor now for almost nine months. In nine months you may have learned another trade" [FWTBT, 260]; "that famous European education that teaches you ... how to find the courage and the right reasons, very valid, very correct reasons, to kill a man who has never done anything to you" [Gary, 273]; "Do you think you have a right to kill?" [FWTBT, 323]; "My beautiful girlfriend is coming. She has legs that begin at her shoulders" [Meyers, 311]; "the victim of his own facile reporting and his novelist's self-absorption, which was heightened by his love affair with Martha" [Meyers, 325]; "I only write once on any one theme; if I don't write it all in one time, it's not worth saying" [Hotchner, 114]. p. 57: "idea of fun ... was a honeymoon on the Burma Road" [Meyers, 356]. p. 60 "based more on fantasy than on fact" [Meyers, 375]; "one of the most decorated non-combatants in military history [of the United States]" [Donaldson, 132]. p. 61: "spelling and syntax" [Meyers, 398]; "true love, [his] last and only and true love" [ARIT, 69].

CHAPTER 3

p. 65: "overdrawn" [quoted in Lynn, 118, emphasis in the original]. p. 66: "Maybe away from Paris I could write about Paris as in Paris I could write about Michigan" [MF, 7]; "If you are lucky enough to have lived in Paris as a young man, then wherever you go for the rest of your life it stays with you, for Paris is a moveable feast" [Hotchner, 57]. p.69: "thinking inside himself that they had done with paint and canvas what he had been striving to do all morning" [Baker, 85]. p. 70: "After writing a story I was always empty and both sad and happy, as though I had made love" [MF, 6]; "But in Paris writing was a new game with Left Bank rules" [Reynolds, 6]; "[T]his is how Paris was in the early days when we were very poor and very happy" [MF, 211]; "[i]t is such an important part of the ethics [of a journalist] that you should never seem to be working" [SAR, 9]; "scum of Greenwich Village, New York, ... skimmed off and deposited in large ladles on that section of Paris adjacent

to the Café Rotonde" [quoted in Reynolds, 24]. p. 71: "she didn't answer, but instead took me to see the lavish new music wing she had built on the house" [Hotchner, 116]. p. 75: "it was a French-English dictionary held upside down" [Baker, 158]. p. 78: "that everything I did not understand probably had something to it" [MF, 18]; "Write the truest sentence you know" [MF, 12]. p. 79: "the career, the career" [Stein, 873]; "egotism and mental laziness versus discipline" [MF, 30]; "Well, Gertrude ... a pronouncement, was a pronouncement, was a pronouncement" [Hotchner, 49]. p. 81: "The girl I was in love with was in Paris then, and I did not take the first train, or the second or the third" [MF, 210]; "All things truly wicked start from an innocence" [MF, 210].

CHAPTER 4

p. 85: "the dream place for a man" [Dupuy, 15]; "I was trying to learn to write, commencing with the simplest things, and one of the simplest things and the most fundamental is violent death" [DIA, 2]; "the whole bullfight is indefensible" [DIA, 1]; "a serious book on such an unmoral subject" [DIA, 4]; "physically or mentally shut his eyes, as one might do if he saw a child that he could not possibly reach or aid, about to be struck by a train" [DIA, 2].
p. 86: "more flamingos! [sic]" [Baker, 111]; "Spain is the only country in which death is a national spectacle" [Lorca, 161]; "are not fascinated by death, its nearness and avoidance. We are fascinated by victory and we replace the avoidance of death by the avoidance of defeat" [DIA, 22]. p. 87: "Bull Gores 2 Yanks Acting As Toreadors" [Dupuy, 82]; "the shadow of a bull's horn" [Leiris, 10]. p. 88: "She was built with curves like the hull of a racing yacht, and you missed none of it with that wool jersey" [SAR, 19]; "Nobody ever lives their lives all the way up except bullfighters" [SAR, 9]; "there is not one local-colored place for tourists in town" [DIA, 51]; "when you can have the Prado and the bullfight season at the same time, with the Fscurial not two hours to the north and Toledo to the south ... it makes you feel badly, all question of immortality aside, to know that you will have to die and never see it again" [DIA, 51]; "because we are human and we live in the dark shadow of death, we experience the frustrated, desperate violence of eroticism" [Bataille, 62]. p. 91: "is performing a work of art and ... is playing with death, bringing it closer, closer, closer to himself, a death that you know is in the horns" [DIA, 213]; "the final sword thrust, the actual encounter between the man and the animal, what the Spanish call the moment of truth" [DIA, 68]; "that flash when man and bull form one figure as the sword goes all the way in" [DIA, 247]; "goes on that way for a while" [MF, 210]; "all stories, if continued far enough, end up in death, and he is no true story-teller who would keep that from you" [DIA, 122]; (caption 2) "I told her about watching the bull, not the horse, when the bulls charged the picadors, and got her watching the picador place the point of his pic" [SAR, 147]; (caption 4) "is an art that deals with death and wipes it out" [DIA, 99]. p. 94: "as a sort of Arabia Deserta ... on tauromachy" [Dupuy, 97]. p. 97 (caption 4) "writing" [DS, 103]. p. 99: "Old wine in its cask sometimes reacts to seasons, and the summer of 1959 was, by Ernest's own avowal, one of the best seasons of his life" [Hotchner, 206]; "Why the hell do the good and brave have to die before everyone else?" [Hotchner, 228].

CHAPTER 5

p. 105: "Never wrote so directly of myself as in ['The Snows of Kilimanjaro']" "as good as I've any right to be" [Hotchner, 161]; "No one has explained what the leopard was seeking at that altitude" [CSS, 39]. p. 107: "this most noisome of diseases, which made every victory a disappointment and converted every minor failure into a catastrophe" [Baker, 250]; "That bastard crosses there of the imagination" [GHA, foreword]. p. 109: "there's nothing wrong with you" [MF, 191]; "poisoned with envy" [GHA, 208]; "inches don't mean anything at all" [GHA, 209]; "spoils everything" [GHA, 210]; "the foreigner destroys" [GHA, 204]; "I would come back to Africa, but not to make a living of it ... I would come back to where it pleased me to live; to really live. Not just let my life pass. Our people went to America because that was the place to go then" [GHA, 204]; "A continent ages quickly once we come" [GHA, 204]; "for we have been there in the books and out of the books — and where we go, if we are any good, there you can go as we have been" [GHA, 79]. p. 110: "you can have, and you want more and more, to have, and be, and live in, to possess now again and always, for that sudden-ended always" [GHA, 53]; "Once they make a purchase" "they only care about box office ... and the last person they value is the writer" [Hotchner, 100]. p. 112: "almost pathetic" [Lynn, 570]; "All this

goddam publicity" [Hotchner, 107]. p. 115: "an African son" [Hotchner, 117]; "black and very beautiful" "absolutely loving and delicate rough" "Anyway she gives me too bad a hard-on" [Lynn, 571]. p. 116: "expressed [his] pleasure at finding that the news of his death had been exaggerated" [Lynn, 572]; "all his contradictory wishes to live and die seem to be contained in the terrible, all-out lunges with which he inflicted another concussion on himself" [Lynn, 572]; "my luck is running good" [Lynn, 572]. p. 118: "appeared to have diminished ... [not] physically diminished, but some of the aura of massiveness seemed to have gone out of him" [Hotchner, 83].

CHAPTER 6

p. 123 "a mixture of Nantucket and New Orleans" "thriving whorehouses" [Meyers, 205]. p. 124: "Fish ... I love you and respect you very much. But I will kill you dead before this day ends" [OMS, 54]. p. 126: "Who ever went ten rounds sitting on his ass?" [Hotchner, 114]; "because people speak like a typewriter works" [Hotchner, 115]; "I've ... never felt better or stronger or healthier in the head or body — nor had better confidence of morale — ... since I've been in America" [Lynn, 377]; "YOUR SONS DAVID AND ANDREW KILLED WITH THEIR MOTHER IN MOTOR ACCIDENT NEAR BIARRITZ ATTENDING TO EVERYTHING PENDING YOUR ARRIVAL DEEPEST SYMPATHY" [IS, 193]; "TRY TO LOCATE ERNEST HEMINGWAY IN NEW YORK ADVISE HIM OF DEATH OF HIS FATHER TODAY ASK HIM TO COMMUNICATE WITH HOME IMMEDIATELY" [Meyers, 209]; "go the same way" [Meyers, 210]. p. 133: "I wish the world wasn't the way it is and that things didn't have to happen to brothers" "I know that if David catches this fish he'll have something inside him for all his life and it will make everything else easier" [IS, 132]; "Oh shit ... you never understand anybody that loves you" [IS, 446]; "Never confuse movement with action" [Hotchner, 26]; "geography isn't any cure for what's the matter with you" [IS, 105]. p. 134: "whoring" [Meyers, 281]. p. 135: "bloody money" "has thrown away and abused his talent" [IS, 105]; "integrity in a writer is like virginity in a woman — once lost, it is never recovered" [Hotchner, 115]. p. 139: "confronted his personal guilt and transformed it into art" [Meyers, 326]; "I'd rather eat monkey manure than die in Key West" [Hotchner, 165]; "stinko deadly lonely" [Baker, 79]. p. 140: "They even thought of taking a picture of Blackie [one of his cats] lying in front of my empty chair, just in case" [Hotchner, 151]; "Writing at its best is a solitary life" "He [the writer] sheds off his loneliness and often his work deteriorates" [Hotchner, 145]. p. 141: "Just as A Moveable Feast portrays the most promising part of his life, so Islands in the Stream depicts the most depressing" [Meyers, 484].

CHAPTER 7

p. 149: "winter of the avalanches" [MF, 207]; "like a happy and innocent winter in childhood" "compared to the next winter, a nightmare winter disguised as the greatest fun of all, and the murderous summer that was to follow" [MF, 207]; "Most of the writing that I did that year was in avalanche time" [MF, 204]; "The wool was natural and the fat had not been removed, and the caps and sweaters and long scarves that Hadley knitted from it never became wet in the snow" [MF, 204]. p. 150: "When I was young I never wanted to get married" "but after I did so, I could never be without a wife again. Same about kids" [Hotchner, 87]; "it isn't fun any more" [CSS, 81]; "All his life a man loved two or three streams better than anything else in the world. Then, he fell in love with a girl and the goddam streams could dry up for all he cared" [Baker, 79]; "the big psychic wound of his life had come when he discovered that his father was a coward" [Baker, 247]; "an All-American bitch" [Baker, 465]. p. 151: "'Oh, shut up and get something to read'" [CSS, 131]; "labels on them from all the hotels where they had spent nights" [CSS, 214]; "Paris and happiness were synonymous" [Hotchner, 48]. p. 153: "This is how Paris was in the early days when we were very poor and very happy" [MF, 211]; "hunger was good discipline" [MF, 67]; "the rich leave everything deader than the roots of any grass Attila's horses' hooves have ever scoured" [MF, 208]; "using the oldest trick there is" [MF, 209].

p. 154: "The wife I had loved first and best and who was the mother of my oldest son ... tonight, in the dream, I slept happily with my true love in my arms" [Donaldson, 150]; "crowning experience of an extraordinary year" [Kert, 58]. p. 155: "The essence of Catherine's tragedy is her unwanted baby" [Meyers, 217]; "whom they finally had to open ... up like a picador's horse" [Hemingway quoted in Meyers, 208]; "Love is that dirty abortive horror that you took me. ... All right, I'm through with you and I'm through with love. Your kind of picknose love. You writer" [HHN, 186]; "Hemingway's mistake was that he thought he had to marry all of them" [Donaldson, 149]; "would require a new woman for each 'big book'" [Donaldson, 165]. p. 159: "was always empty and both sad and happy, as though I had made love" [MF, 6]; "to interrupt a man while he [is] writing a book ... [is] as bad as to interrupt a man when he [is] in bed making love" [Hotchner, 147]; "he who lives by the sword dies by the sword!" [Donaldson, 164]; "a glass of hemlock" [Hotchner, 87]; "the most beautiful woman ever to visit the White House" [Meyers, 242]; "the more intense Hemingway's passion was in life, the greater his expression of hatred in his fiction" [Meyers, 253]. p. 162: "last and only and true love" [ARIT, 69]; "in restoring Ernest's writing vigor" [Hotchner, 177]; "sparked the jerky graph of his heart" [Meyers, 441].

CHAPTEr 8

p. 169: "[I]f a man sought death all his life, could he not have found her before the age of fifty-four?" [quoted in Donaldson, 282]; "that old whore" [Donaldson, 282]; "autographed everything from Of Human Bondage to Casserole Cookery" "Must be the goddamn beard" [Hotchner, 106–107]; "I should have stayed in that second kite [plane] in Butiaba" [Hotchner, 109]; "I had a nice private life before ... and now I feel like somebody crapped in it and wiped themselves on slick paper and left it there" [Hotchner, 109]. p. 170: "published a huge volume of ... letters, some of them very, very personal" [Hotchner, XI]; "would one day write a book exposing the paranoid behavior of his last years, he would have killed him — perhaps not ... personally, but seen to it he was disposed of in an automobile accident, say, or out on the Gulf Stream" [Donaldson, 217]; "the shyest man [he] had ever photographed," "a wall of silence and myth" [Donaldson, 189]. p. 172: "victims of unsynchronized passion" (caption) [Hotchner, 26]. p. 175: "[I] refuse to read any reviews on Across the River, not for blood pressure but they are about as interesting and constructive as reading other people's laundry lists" [Hotchner, 69]; "triste métier" [ARIT, 184]; "You know the real métier triste? ... Writing. There's a real métier triste" for you" [Hotchner, 118]; "writing is the only thing that makes me feel I'm not wasting my time sticking around" [Hotchner, 144]; "You should always write your best against dead writers ... and beat them one by one. Why do you want to fight Dostoevsky in your first fight?" [quoted in Meyers, 464–65]. p. 178: "in no shape for this tougher Prize-combat" [Hotchner, 143]; "Writing, at its best, is a lonely life. ... He grows in public stature as he sheds his loneliness and often his work deteriorates" [Hotchner, 145]. p. 179: "Sic transit hijo de puta" [Meyers, 518]. p. 181: "secret place [CSS, 515]; "an irritating son of a bitch" [Meyers, 282]; "that no-one was allowed to touch his head" [Meyers, 529]; "a vague resemblance to some of the pale noble ladies painted by Goya" [Meyers, 531]; "without benefit of the Havana customs" [Hotchner, 246]. p. 186: "would sometimes stand at the gun rack of rifles, holding one of the guns, staring out of the window at the distant mountains" [Hotchner, 274]; "Ernest's general condition as depression-persecutory" [Hotchner, 275]; "what is the sense of ruining my head and erasing my memory, which is my capital, and putting me out of business?" [Hotchner, 279–80]; "This wonderful damn book, I can't finish it ... (caption 1) Not this fall or next spring or in ten years from now. I can't." [Hotchner, 286]; "true to his own identity" [Hotchner, 119]. p. 187: "those admirable American instruments so easily carried, so sure of effect, so well designed to end the American dream when it becomes a nightmare, their only drawback is the mess they leave for relatives to clean up" [HHN, 238]; "no sign of disorder or stain" [Meyers, 561]; "Old as I am, I continue to be amazed at the sudden emergence of daffodils and of stories" [Hotchner, 163].

Opposite page:
Cuba, 1940.

Original Editions of Hemingway's Works

Three Stories and Ten Poems,
Paris and Dijon, Contact Publishing Company, 1923.

In Our Time,
Paris, Three Mountains Press, 1924.

In Our Time,
New York, Boni & Liveright, 1925.

The Torrents of Spring,
New York, Charles Scribner's Sons, 1926.

The Sun Also Rises,
New York, Charles Scribner's Sons, 1926.

Today Is Friday,
Englewood, New Jersey, The As Stable Publications, 1926.

Men Without Women,
New York, Charles Scribner's Sons, 1927.

A Farewell to Arms,
New York, Charles Scribner's Sons, 1929.

In Our Time,
New York, Charles Scribner's Sons, 1930.
This edition features an introduction by Edmund Wilson (which includes "On the Quay at Smyrna").

Death in the Afternoon,
New York, Charles Scribner's Sons, 1932.

Winner Take Nothing,
New York, Charles Scribner's Sons, 1933.

God Rest You Merry, Gentlemen,
New York, the House of Books Limited, 1933.

Green Hills of Africa,
New York, Charles Scribner's Sons, 1935.

To Have and Have Not,
New York, Charles Scribner's Sons, 1935.

The Spanish Earth,
Cleveland, J. B. Savage Company, 1938.

The Fifth Column and the First Forty-Nine Stories,
New York, Charles Scribner's Sons, 1938.

For Whom the Bell Tolls,
New York, Charles Scribner's Sons, 1940.

Men at War,
New York, Crown Publishers, 1942.

Opposite page:
Ernest, around 1960.

The Portable Hemingway,
Malcolm Cowley, editor, New York, The Viking Press, 1944.

The Essential Hemingway,
London, Jonathan Cape, 1947.

Across the River and Into the Trees,
New York, Charles Scribner's Sons, 1950.

The Old Man and the Sea,
New York, Charles Scribner's Sons, 1952.

The Hemingway Reader,
New York, Charles Scribner's Sons, 1953.

Collected Poems,
San Francisco, 1960 (unauthorized edition).

The Snows of Kilimanjaro,
New York, Charles Scribner's Sons, 1961.

Hemingway: The Wild Years,
New York, Dell, 1962 (articles from 1920 to 1924).

A Moveable Feast,
New York, Charles Scribner's Sons, 1964.

By-line: Ernest Hemingway. Selected Articles and Dispatches of Four Decades,
William White, editor, New York, Charles Scribner's Sons, 1967.

Ernest Hemingway, Cub Reporter,
Matthew J. Bruccoli, editor, Pittsburgh, University of Pittsburgh Press, 1970.

Islands in the Stream,
New York, Charles Scribner's Sons, 1970.

The Nick Adams Stories,
New York, Charles Scribner's Sons, 1972.

88 Poems,
Nicholas Gerogiannis, editor, New York and London, Harcourt Brace Jovanovich/Bruccoli Clark, 1979.

Ernest Hemingway: Selected Letters 1917–1961,
Carlos Baker, editor, New York, Charles Scribner's Sons, 1981.

The Garden of Eden,
New York, Charles Scribner's Sons, 1986.

The Complete Short Stories of Ernest Hemingway: The Finca Vigía Edition,
New York, Charles Scribner's Sons, 1987.

Complete Poems,
Nicholas Gerogiannis, editor, University of Nebraska Press, 1992.

Ernest, dressed as a little girl, plays in front of the family home in 1905.

The Ernest Hemingway Collection

JFK Library, Boston – Public domain

Except:

Gamma (pp. 10: Jean-Philippe Charbonnier; 171: Yousuf Karsh). Aude/Wikimedia Commons (p. 18 btm right). Robert Capa/International Center of Photography/Magnum Photos (pp. 52 btm, 53 btm right, 54 top, 55 top, 156–157, 158). Mencken (p. 56 right). AKG-Images (pp. 65: Joan Miró, La Masia, 1921–22, Washington National Gallery, Oronoz; 122; 177). Rue des Archives (pp. 66 btm and center, 67, 69 top, 70 top, 131 top: Suddeutsche Zeitung; 140 btm left: The Granger Collection). Rodero (pp. 84, 86 center). Cano Madrid (pp. 95 top, 100 btm left, 180, 181 top). Cuevas (pp. 96 top left, btm right; 100 right). Fournol (pp. 95 btm, 101). Burrows (pp. 96 btm left, 97). Burke (p. 98 btm left). Hotchner (pp. 99 btm, 100 upper left). Earl Theisen (pp. 102, 108, 110, 111, 112 left and btm, 114, 115 except right). Hemis.fr (p. 130 top and right). Getty Images (pp. 6: Deborah Jaffe/Contour; 130 btm left, 131 btm, 179 btm right: Sven Creutzmann/Mambo Photo; 170 right: Bob Landry; 170 btm: Lloyd Arnold; 172, 186: Hulton Archive; 174: Peter Stackpole; 176 top: Alfred Eisenstaedt; 176 btm left: Earl Theisen; 178 top: American Stock Archive; 179 top: Ker Robertson; 182 right: John Bryson; 187 top: Francis Miller). AFP (p. 179 btm left). Leavens (p. 142 right). Paul Radkai (p. 142 btm left). Malmberg (pp. 144–145). Arnold (pp. 148, 159 btm left). Hamon (p. 160 top left). Scribner's (p. 162 top). Verruzzi (p. 159 btm left). Bryson (pp. 165, 183, 184–185).

Opposite page:
1959. Ordóñez takes a picture of Ernest —
who is taking a picture of him!

In my country we say thank you.
René Char

We never write alone. Particularly when telling the life story of a man like Ernest Hemingway — even if there is only one author to such an enterprise, it can only be a work of collective memory and narrative. Hemingway comes to us through his writing, which is what distinguishes him from the millions of other men of his time who lived, suffered, fought, loved, hoped and despaired just as he did. We may sometimes be moved by their story, but, more often, it leaves us indifferent. Ernest Hemingway is the product of his work; he is also the character handed down to us by both academic and popular culture and those who have preserved it. Whoever writes about "Hemingway" bears a huge debt to his biographers, who for more than half a century have pieced together this character for us, and to his children and grandchildren, who bring us the testimony of those who experienced the fiction of the man in their own lives. The emotion of sharing the cover of this book with Mariel, one of his granddaughters, cannot easily be put into words. Honor is one thing, and the principled feeling of undertaking a joint enterprise in a common cause is another, even more precious. This book would not have seen the light of day without the enormous task that the biographies of Carlos Baker, Jeffrey Meyers, Kenneth Lynn, Scott Donaldson, Peter Griffin, Michael Reynolds and Bernice Kert all represent, as well as the memoirs of those who shared Hemingway's life, like Mary Hemingway, Valerie Hemingway and Aaron Hotchner. Few other 20th-century authors have inspired so much passion on the part of the learned and the literary; an entire volume would not be enough to cite all the works devoted to the man who takes us to other places with his writing. This present work does not aim to offer a close reading of Hemingway's work, but its chapters are nonetheless informed by the hundreds of articles and books of criticism that Hemingway's writing has inspired. The present work also, and above all, is the fruit of more than a decade of visiting Hemingway's work, as well as conferences, courses and seminars (attended and given), research, innumerable articles and interminable conversations in Ernest's stomping grounds of Oak Park, Paris, Key West, Madrid, Ronda, Lausanne and Stresa; I owe a debt of gratitude to all the assiduous, passionate readers of Hemingway, and I extend my deep and sincere thanks to them. The Hemingway Foundation and Society organizes a biannual conference in the locations where Hemingway lived and worked: the most recent was held in Lausanne, Switzerland, under the title "Hemingway's Extreme Geographies." The support of members of this scholarly yet friendly organization — particularly Suzanne del Gizzo, Michael Federspiel, Kirk Curnutt, James Meredith, E.H. Stoneback, Allan Josephs and Carl Eby — has been vital to me, as has the JFK Library in Boston and Susan Wrynn, the curator of the Hemingway Collection, and her colleagues Laurie Austin, Maryrose Grossman and Marti Verso. I could not have written this book without the physical and moral support of the University of Lausanne, whose students force me to read more closely, and the colleagues who have helped and supported me during the whole period of the writing of this book. My thanks go also to the editorial team of Michel Lafon, who have worked miracles in getting this project off the ground. And, finally, my thanks to my family and friends, who put up with me and encouraged me when I most needed it: without them this book would not now be elsewhere — in the hands of the dear reader.

B.V.

Opposite page:
Ernest in 1944.

Publisher's Credits

Karyn Dilworth, Lela Buttery,

Michael Katakis, Yessenia Santos, Isabelle Weygand,

James H. Meredith, Kirk Curnutt, Geneviève Hily-Mane,

Peter Riva,

Susan Wrynn, Laurie Austin, Marti Verso, Maryrose Grossman, Sara Ludovissy,

Norman Aberle, Muriel Feiner, Roxie Livingston, Scott Bryson, Jean Chabaud,

Elsa Lafon-Goldstein and Jonah Goldstein,

Bernadette and Daniel Delhomme.

Editorial Director
Édouard Boulon-Cluzel

Design
Mathieu Thauvin